Chef Essentials

Discover how to deploy software, manage hosts, and
scale your infrastructure with Chef

John Ewart

[PACKT] open source
PUBLISHING   community experience distilled

BIRMINGHAM - MUMBAI

Chef Essentials

First published: September 2014

Production reference: 1190914

Published by Packt Publishing Ltd.
Livery Place
35 Livery Street
Birmingham B3 2PB, UK.

ISBN 978-1-78398-304-9

www.packtpub.com

Cover image by Prashant Timappa Shetty (sparkling.spectrum.123@gmail.com)

Credits

Author

John Ewart

Reviewers

Joshua Black

Lauren Malhoit

Eric Maxey

Commissioning Editor

Edward Gordon

Acquisition Editor

Llewellyn Rozario

Content Development Editor

Govindan K

Technical Editor

Shubhangi Dhamgaye

Copy Editors

Roshni Banerjee

Mradula Hegde

Gladson Monteiro

Project Coordinator

Sageer Parkar

Proofreaders

Simran Bhogal

Maria Gould

Ameesha Green

Linda Morris

Indexer

Rekha Nair

Production Coordinator

Arvindkumar Gupta

Cover Work

Arvindkumar Gupta

About the Author

John Ewart is a system architect, software developer, and lecturer. He has designed and taught courses at a variety of institutions, including the University of California, The California State University, and local community colleges. These courses cover a wide range of computer science topics, including Java, data structures and algorithms, operating systems fundamentals, Unix and Linux system administration, and web application development. In addition to working and teaching, he maintains and contributes to a number of open source projects. He currently resides in Redmond, Washington, with his wife, Mary, and their two children.

About the Reviewers

Joshua Black has been working with computers professionally for 20 years. He has a wide range of experience and expertise, which includes systems and network administration, mobile app development, and production web applications. He earned a BS degree in Computer Science with a minor in Math from California State University, Chico, in 2005. He currently resides in Chico, California, with his wife, Rachel, and their four children.

Lauren Malhoit has been in the field of IT for over 10 years and has acquired several data center certifications. She's currently a technical virtualization architect, specializing in virtualization and storage in data center. She has been writing for a few years for TechRepublic, TechRepublic Pro, and VirtualizationSoftware. As a Cisco Champion, EMC Elect, VMware vExpert, and PernixPro, she stays involved in the community. She also hosts a bi-weekly technology podcast called AdaptingIT (http://www.adaptingit.com/). She has been a delegate for Tech Field Day several times as well. She recently published her first book, *VMware vCenter Operations Manager Essentials*, *Packt Publishing*.

Eric Maxey has a varied background in writing software, including making console video games and analyzing the ad revenue data. He ran a small business that pioneered a new kind of bitcoin mining pool, which has now become something of a standard. When not jacked into the metaverse, he likes to work on electric bicycles and ride them offroad.

www.PacktPub.com

Support files, eBooks, discount offers and more

You might want to visit www.PacktPub.com for support files and downloads related to your book.

Did you know that Packt offers eBook versions of every book published, with PDF and ePub files available? You can upgrade to the eBook version at www.PacktPub.com and as a print book customer, you are entitled to a discount on the eBook copy. Get in touch with us at service@packtpub.com for more details.

At www.PacktPub.com, you can also read a collection of free technical articles, sign up for a range of free newsletters and receive exclusive discounts and offers on Packt books and eBooks.

http://PacktLib.PacktPub.com

Do you need instant solutions to your IT questions? PacktLib is Packt's online digital book library. Here, you can access, read and search across Packt's entire library of books.

Why Subscribe?

- Fully searchable across every book published by Packt
- Copy and paste, print and bookmark content
- On demand and accessible via web browser

Free Access for Packt account holders

If you have an account with Packt at www.PacktPub.com, you can use this to access PacktLib today and view nine entirely free books. Simply use your login credentials for immediate access.

Table of Contents

Preface

Chef is an indispensable tool to manage your infrastructure. It consists of a set of tools that are designed to work together to enable you to model and manage your systems. This is a large space to fill, and Chef provides you with the tools to do this in a very flexible and powerful way. It achieves this through a combination of services, end host agents, a web interface, and command-line tools that work in unison to deliver an incredible suite of tools.

Chef's services are responsible for storing, managing, and distributing data about your infrastructure through an API. Endhost software agents that run on nodes (managed systems) are responsible for performing updates to systems, and the web interface, along with command-line tools, allows an administrator to edit and consume information that is vended by the API service.

One of the most attractive features of Chef is that you can leverage its API to easily integrate existing tools, or you can develop new tools to meet specific needs. Any organization with a moderate number of developer resources can harness the power of Chef to manage their systems. For example, one can easily build software to import data from Chef into a reporting tool of some form and dynamically reconfigure infrastructure based on a third-party tool's output—the sky's the limit. This is incredibly valuable to anybody who has an existing infrastructure because it provides a convenient path to integrate Chef into their environment.

There are a number of ways to access Chef. The quickest way for a single user to manage his/her infrastructure (virtual machines, a handful of hosts, and so on) is to use Chef-solo, a product geared towards single-user environments. In a small environment, setting up a hosted server is a good way to manage infrastructure automation among team members. If you need to, you can configure the hosted environment as a highly available system using load balancers and other technologies. Alternatively, if hosting the service yourself is not an option, you can use hosted Chef, a software-as-a-service (SaaS) model, thus paying for access to a hosted service.

Configuration management software was created to fill a need—managing infrastructure is a challenging task. Regardless of the scale you operate on, keeping track of software versions, upgrading systems, and generating consistent configuration data is a lot of work. It is tempting to update a configuration file on one system, only to forget to commit those changes somewhere, or to apply them to existing or future hosts. This is very convenient, but it quickly leads to inconsistency between hosts. When you are working with only one or two hosts, this may be acceptable. As such, a system grows from a few servers to dozens, hundreds, or possibly thousands—this type of system management does not scale due to time requirements and configuration errors that result from size and complexity.

Consider a scenario where you are migrating a database server to a new host. This would involve: bringing up a new host, installing all of the required software on your list to ensure it has parity with the old server (you did keep a list, right?), ensuring that your database server was configured with the same options, putting the correct firewall rules in place, tuning the filesystem, setting up monitoring tools, updating DNS records or changing web application configurations to point to the new host, and so on. Now imagine that, instead of one server in one data center, you have 10 database servers in 10 data centers, each with their own IP ranges, hardware configurations, and networking rules. Situations such as this are exactly why system configuration management software packages were developed: to make the lives of system administrators and engineers much easier.

This scenario, and many others like it, is where Chef is indispensable. Having the ability to describe your hosts, configuration data, and roles, and then apply that across as many hosts as you like means that you can manage large fleets of hosts just as easily as you can manage one or two.

What this book covers

Chapter 1, Installing Chef, introduces you to the architecture of Chef, various installation methods, and a guide to setting up Chef (solo and self-hosted). It includes information on using hosted Chef (and what that means for your team) and Vagrant with Chef-solo.

Chapter 2, Modeling Your Infrastructure, introduces how to model your infrastructure with Chef using your newly installed system. This chapter will cover modeling environments, small and large, as well as how to integrate with cloud technologies using Chef (AWS, Rackspace Cloud, and so on).

Chapter 3, Integrating with the Cloud, covers how Chef helps you scale your infrastructure using any combination of physical, virtual, and cloud-hosted systems. This chapter discusses how to use Chef to provision and manage hosts using cloud providers as easily as your local systems including AWS and Rackspace Cloud.

Chapter 4, Working with Cookbooks, covers how every Chef needs cookbooks — once your systems are part of your Chef-managed fleet, you can begin collecting, developing, and applying recipes to your hosts. It includes in-depth explanations of the structure and development of cookbooks and recipes, as well as how to test, publish, and share them.

Chapter 5, Testing Your Recipes, focuses on one compelling reason to use Chef to configure your infrastructure, that is, recipes are written in Ruby code and can be tested as any program would be tested. Here, you will learn how to test your recipes through a variety of testing mechanisms.

Chapter 6, From Development to Deployment, covers how to take a custom application from development to a production deployment with Chef. It contains a complete example that includes provisioning a web server, database server, and users as well as deploying code from source control.

Chapter 7, Beyond Basic Recipes and Cookbooks, delves into developing extensions to Chef through advanced concepts, including custom providers and resource types, using the Chef search engine, advanced scripting, and more.

Chapter 8, Extras You Need to Know, expands your knowledge of how to leverage Chef for infrastructure automation, complex systems integration, and securely storing and distributing sensitive data with Chef.

What you need for this book

This book assumes that you are familiar with at least one programming language (it does not need to be a compiled language, and knowledge of an interpreted language will be suitable. Chef uses Ruby for its dynamic, scriptable components and any experience with Ruby will be valuable. However, having a strong understanding of program logic will provide you with the background to be productive with Chef.

For those who are not experts with Ruby, there will be a wide array of example listings that can be copied directly and executed as part of the book's offerings. This will enable you to use the examples without any previous Ruby experience. However, a working knowledge of Ruby will be needed in order to expand on the book's code examples or while writing your own recipes from scratch.

You will be walked through the steps required to install Chef on a Linux-based host. In order to be immediately successful, you will need administrative access to a host that runs a modern version of Linux; Ubuntu 13.10 is what will be used for demonstration purposes. If you are a more experienced reader, then a recent release of almost any distribution will work just as well (but you may be required to do a little bit of extra work that is not outlined in the book). If you do not have access to a dedicated Linux host, a virtual host (or hosts), running inside of virtualization software, such as VirtualBox will work.

Additionally, you will need access to the Internet to download software packages that you do not already have, as well as an installation of the Ruby programming language Version 1.9 or higher.

Who this book is for

This book targets developers and system administrators who need to manage infrastructure and are looking to automate their system management. This includes infrastructure ranging in size from small-scale installations with a handful of hosts to multicontinent corporate IT systems with hundreds or even thousands of hosts. Anybody whose job involves maintaining systems will benefit from the concepts being covered.

Conventions

In this book, you will find a number of styles of text that distinguish between different kinds of information. Here are some examples of these styles, and an explanation of their meaning.

Code words in text, database table names, folder names, filenames, file extensions, pathnames, dummy URLs, user input, and Twitter handles are shown as follows: "The search method has a similar format to the knife command."

A block of code is set as follows:

```
all_users = search(:users, 'id:*')
users_s = search(:users, 'id:s*')
all_nodes = search(:node, '*')
```

Any command-line input or output is written as follows:

```
$ knife data bag show credentials aws
```

New terms and **important words** are shown in bold. Words that you see on the screen, in menus or dialog boxes for example, appear in the text like this: "Once there, a tab labeled **Chef Server** will be present at the top of the page."

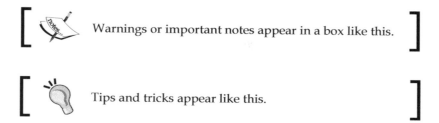

[Warnings or important notes appear in a box like this.]

[Tips and tricks appear like this.]

Reader feedback

Feedback from our readers is always welcome. Let us know what you think about this book—what you liked or may have disliked. Reader feedback is important for us to develop titles that you really get the most out of.

To send us general feedback, simply send an e-mail to feedback@packtpub.com, and mention the book title via the subject of your message.

If there is a topic that you have expertise in and you are interested in either writing or contributing to a book, see our author guide on www.packtpub.com/authors.

Customer support

Now that you are the proud owner of a Packt book, we have a number of things to help you to get the most from your purchase.

Errata

Although we have taken every care to ensure the accuracy of our content, mistakes do happen. If you find a mistake in one of our books—maybe a mistake in the text or the code—we would be grateful if you would report this to us. By doing so, you can save other readers from frustration and help us improve subsequent versions of this book. If you find any errata, please report them by visiting http://www.packtpub.com/submit-errata, selecting your book, clicking on the **errata submission form** link, and entering the details of your errata. Once your errata are verified, your submission will be accepted and the errata will be uploaded on our website, or added to any list of existing errata, under the Errata section of that title. Any existing errata can be viewed by selecting your title from http://www.packtpub.com/support.

Piracy

Piracy of copyright material on the Internet is an ongoing problem across all media. At Packt, we take the protection of our copyright and licenses very seriously. If you come across any illegal copies of our works, in any form, on the Internet, please provide us with the location address or website name immediately so that we can pursue a remedy.

Please contact us at copyright@packtpub.com with a link to the suspected pirated material.

We appreciate your help in protecting our authors, and our ability to bring you valuable content.

Questions

You can contact us at questions@packtpub.com if you are having a problem with any aspect of the book, and we will do our best to address it.

1
Installing Chef

Before you can start using Chef, you will need to install it. Here you will find a guide to install Chef, and because Chef requires Ruby, some Ruby concepts as well. This chapter discusses the following:

- Key terminology and concepts related to Chef
- An overview of Chef's architecture
- Working with Ruby gems
- Installing chef-solo (a local-only engine to use Chef)
- A brief example on using chef-solo
- Installing the Chef server on your own host
- Verifying your Chef installation

Terminology

As with any other technology, Chef has its own terminology. As you will see, Chef's nomenclature is a mix of technological terms (nodes, workstations, servers, roles, and so on) and cooking terms (cookbooks, recipes, and so on). There are three primary actors that we are concerned with at this point: nodes, the Chef service, and workstations.

- **Node**: A node is a client that applies roles and recipes, as described by the administrator in the Chef service (that is, a server in your environment that is being configured via Chef). These are the consumers of the configuration, the elements of your infrastructure. They can be physical or virtual machines and can run on Linux, Windows, or technically any other system that is capable of running Ruby (some systems may not be supported out of the box by Chef).

- **Chef service**: The Chef service is a multicomponent system that combines several services to provide its functionality. The primary functional components are an API service, full-text searching via Solr, persistent storage using PostgreSQL, and RabbitMQ for interservice communication. Additionally, there is a web interface that provides a graphical tool to manage system data. Clients (nodes) use the API service to determine which roles and recipes to apply, and `knife` (a command-line tool) uses the API to allow an administrator to edit and manage their Chef configuration.

- **Workstation**: A workstation is a host that is used to issue commands. A workstation can be a separate host outside of your Chef service installation, a managed node, or the server that the Chef components are running on. There are a variety of command-line tools that are provided to interact with the service, which will be installed onto your workstation(s).

- **Recipe**: A recipe is a script that describes a set of steps to take to achieve a specific goal. As an example, a recipe might describe how to deploy your custom software, provision a database, or add a host to a load balancer.

- **Cookbook**: A cookbook is a collection of recipes that are used to collectively describe how to install, configure, and manage various aspects of your infrastructure. For example, a cookbook might describe how to provision MySQL, PostgreSQL or Apache, manage users, install printers, or perform any other system tasks.

Working with Chef

For single user setups, chef-solo is a version of the chef-client that allows you to use Chef without requiring access to a server. Chef-solo runs locally and requires that a cookbook and any of its dependencies be present on the node being managed. As a result, chef-solo provides a limited subset of the full chef server mode of operation. Most of the features that chef-solo is missing revolve around search and centralized data management, which are not critical for managing virtual machines or a small collection of nodes. The installation and maintenance is simple, but the feature set is smaller.

Installing the Chef server will give you access to the full set of Chef functionality. This mode requires access to a Linux-based host that is network-accessible by the nodes and workstations that will interact with the system. Thanks to the recent effort from the folks at Chef (formerly Opscode), the process of installing Chef has been greatly simplified. The benefits of this installation model are that you get centralized management, search, user authentication, and such, but at the cost of managing your own service.

If you need the features of Chef but do not want to maintain your own server, hosted Chef is a great option for you. Hosted Chef (`https://manage.opscode.com/signup`) gives you all the features of a self-hosted Chef but without having to worry about upgrades, extra hardware, or system availability. For a small infrastructure (up to five hosts), hosted Chef is free and a great way to get started. Beyond this, plans have a monthly fee, and the price will vary according to the number of hosts you want to manage.

Installing chef-solo

Chef-solo is designed for individuals who do not need a hosted installation for a large-scale infrastructure management. Typical use cases of chef-solo include developers managing virtual machines, test installations, or small-scale infrastructure management. The installation of chef-solo is as simple as installing a single Ruby gem.

The Ruby gem

For those who are not intimately familiar with Ruby, a Ruby gem is a mechanism to package, deliver, and manage Ruby code. These packages may be libraries that provide functionality for developers, or they may be composed only of scripts and tools. Chef-solo is, like many things in life, somewhere in the middle. The gem contains a set of libraries that make up the core functionality as well as a suite of scripts that are used by end users. Before you install Chef, you should consider installing **Ruby Version Manager** (**RVM**), rbenv, chruby, or another Ruby manager of your choice to keep your gem collections isolated.

Managing gems

A great tool to manage your gems is RVM. The simplest way to install RVM is to use the installation script provided by the development team on the RVM website (`http://rvm.io`). The following command will download the script and pipe it through bash:

```
curl -sSL https://get.rvm.io | bash -s stable
```

Once it is installed, you will initially need to include RVM's functionality in your shell:

```
source ~/.rvm/scripts/rvm
```

Additionally, you might need to add the previous command line to your shell's startup scripts (such as ~/.bashrc or ~/.zshrc, depending on which shell you use). Once RVM is installed, you will want to install a recent version of Ruby, for example, Ruby 1.9.3:

```
rvm install 1.9.3
```

Once Ruby 1.9 is installed, you will want to create a **gemset**. A gemset is RVM's way of isolating gems inside a container, and it will provide you with a place to install gems in such a way that they will not conflict with other gems. This has the benefit of allowing you to install anything you want, without requiring administrative privileges and keeping gems from conflicting with each other. A gemset can be created using the following command:

```
rvm use 1.9.3@chef --create
```

The previous command will simultaneously create the gemset named chef (if it does not exist) for your installation of Ruby 1.9.3 and then set it as the active gemset. Once you start using this new gemset, you will want to install the Chef gem—this contains chef-solo and all the command-line tools you need to work with Chef—using the gem command-line tool:

```
gem install chef
```

Verifying that chef-solo works

Now that the Chef gem is installed, it is time to verify that everything is working fine. In order to use chef-solo, you need to give the following information to it:

- What recipes to apply by providing a run list in a file named node.json
- What the recipes are—these are stored in cookbooks that are found in the cookbooks directory
- How to find the cookbooks and the run list via a file named solo.rb

For simplicity, we will store all of these files inside of the chef directory in your home directory. You are free to put things where you see fit as you become more comfortable working with Chef.

In order to exercise our new tool, we will do something simple: we'll write a recipe that will create an example.txt file in your home directory. The recipe we create will be called create_file, and we'll put that recipe inside a cookbook, which will be named demo.

First, create the directory that will contain the demo cookbook's recipes (and any in between):

```
user@host:~ $ mkdir -p ~/chef/cookbooks/demo/recipes
```

Next, add the following code to a file, create_file.rb, located in the demo cookbook directory you created at ~/chef/cookbooks/demo/recipes:

```
file "#{ENV['HOME']}/example.txt" do
  action :create
  content "Greetings #{ENV['USER']}!"
end
```

This tells Chef that we want to create a file, $HOME/example.txt. Its contents should be Greetings $USER, where $USER will be replaced with the value of $USER, typically the login name of whoever is executing the recipe.

 For those unfamiliar, UNIX (and Windows as well) uses environment variables as a mechanism to exchange data between processes. Some environment variables are set when the user logs in to the system such as HOME, USER, and a variety of others. These variables are available in Ruby using the ENV hash, where the keys are the variable names. In a UNIX shell, these are accessed using the $ prefix. So, the user's home is referred to as $HOME in the shell and ENV['HOME'] inside Ruby.

Now we will need to create a JSON document that describes what chef-solo should execute. JSON is an acronym for JavaScript Object Notation, and Chef uses JSON extensively because it is easy to parse, human readable, and easy to generate from all sorts of tools and languages. Create a file, node.json, located in our work directory (~/chef/ in this case) and add the following content in order to tell Chef that we want to execute the newly created create_file recipe in the demo cookbook:

```
{
    "run_list": [
        "recipe[demo::create_file]"
    ]
}
```

Here, we are defining the node as having a run list, which is just an array of things to do, and that the run list contains one recipe, create_file, which it can find in the demo cookbook (the general form of a recipe being **cookbook::recipe**).

Finally, we'll tell Chef where to find the files we just created using a `solo.rb` file that we will store in our working directory (`~/chef` in our case):

```
CHEF_ROOT="#{ENV['HOME']}/chef"
file_cache_path "#{CHEF_ROOT}"
cookbook_path "#{CHEF_ROOT}/cookbooks"
json_attribs "#{CHEF_ROOT}/node.json"
```

Now that you have populated the required configuration files, you can run chef-solo and execute the run list specified. In our case, the run list is defined as only one recipe, `create_file`, but can be as simple or as complex as needed. The previous configuration tells Chef to load the node configuration from the file `node.json` to look for cookbooks in `~/chef/cookbooks/` and to store any state data in `~/chef/`. In order to execute these commands, you will want to run chef-solo:

```
chef-solo -c ~/chef/solo.rb
```

The `-c` option tells chef-solo which script contains the configuration. Once you do this, you will see the actions that your recipe is performing:

```
Starting Chef Client, version 11.8.2

Compiling Cookbooks...

Converging 1 resources

Recipe: demo::create_file

  * file[/home/user/example.txt] action create

    - create new file /home/user/example.txt

    - update content in file /home/user/example.txt from none to b4a3cc

        --- /home/user/example.txt        2014-01-20 23:59:54.692819000
-0500

        +++ /tmp/.example.txt20140122-13411-1vxtg7v    2014-01-20
23:59:54.692819000 -0500

        @@ -1 +1,2 @@

        +Greetings user!


Chef Client finished, 1 resources updated
```

Once it is completed, you will see that `~/example.txt` contains the greeting that you defined in the recipe. Now that you have successfully used chef-solo, let's move on to the Chef service.

Installing a Chef server

If your team needs to have centralized infrastructure management and does not want to use a hosted platform, then a self-installed Chef server is a perfect fit. This installation guide assumes that you will be running the Chef server on a supported Linux-based system.

The Chef service components can be installed on a single machine without any issue. Installing it on a single host will limit your ability to scale or be highly available, but will provide a very simple path to getting started with the Chef service.

Requirements and recent changes

Since the Chef service is designed to be a multiuser platform and provides functionalities that chef-solo does not offer, the installation is more complex and involves more software to achieve this functionality. Services such as Solr for full-text indexing and PostgreSQL for data storage can be a significant resource for consumers, so you will want to install Chef on a host with sufficient memory and disk space. A system with 2 GB of memory and 5-10 GB of disk space available will be plenty for a small to medium sized installation. You will need more resources as your requirements for data storage and indexing increase over time, so plan accordingly.

Additionally, for those who have installed the Chef server before, the installation path has been greatly simplified. In addition to replacing CouchDB with PostgreSQL as the primary data storage engine, there is now a single **omnibus** installation package for Chef that installs all of the requirements for Chef at a single location so that it operates in isolation and does not require dependencies to be installed separately.

Installation requirements

In order to install the Chef service, you will need to have the following:

- A system running a supported Linux variant (64 bit Ubuntu Linux 10.04 through 12.10 or 64 bit Red Hat Enterprise Linux 5 or 6)—this can be physical or virtual. If you do not have the local resources for this, AWS or RackSpace cloud servers are good options.
- A network connection to the host in order to download the installer.
- Administrative privileges (using sudo or direct root access) on the host where you are installing the services.
- Enough free space on the host to perform the download and installation (minimum 500 MB, including the download, but 1 GB to 2 GB is preferred).

What you will be installing

At the end of this section, you will have a fully functional Chef service installed and ready to work with. Before you get started, let's look at what you will be installing on your system so that you know what to expect. The components that make up a Chef service are as follows:

- The Chef API service
- Message queue (AMQP)
- Data storage
- Search service
- Web-based management console

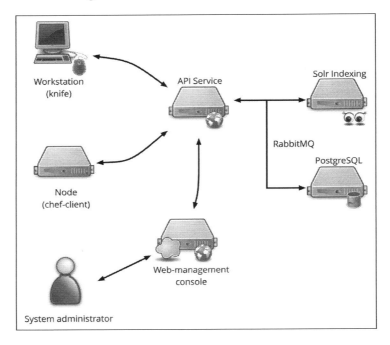

The Chef API service is responsible for delivering run lists and receiving information from nodes as well as providing a way for a system administrator to configure recipes, run lists, data bags, and the like. In order to generate this data, the API service relies on its persistent data storage engine, in this case PostgreSQL, to store its data. The option to search for data is provided by the Solr search engine, and RabbitMQ is responsible for gluing them all together. Together, these components provide Chef with the ability to distribute, store, index, and manage your infrastructure's configuration data.

Getting the installer

The easiest way to install Chef is through a single downloadable package, which is provided for Ubuntu 10.04 through 12.10 and Red Hat Enterprise Linux Versions 5 and 6. This package, referred to as the **omnibus** installer, contains everything you need to get a server up and running. You can find it on `http://www.getchef.com/chef/install/`.

At the time of writing this, 11.0.10 is the latest version and is the one that will be used for this book. The newer version of the 11.x series of Chef should have a very similar, if not identical, configuration. Note that these installers are somewhat large, being that they contain all of the dependencies needed. For example, the Ubuntu 12.10 package for Chef 11.0.10 is approximately 200 MB in size.

 Although these are the officially supported distributions and releases, it is entirely possible that these installers will work on different but compatible distributions. It may be possible, for example, to use CentOS instead of Red Hat Enterprise Linux or Debian instead of Ubuntu. However, these will most likely require some manual dependency resolutions and may not work without a lot of effort (and even then, possibly not at all).

Installation outline

Installation on all supported platforms is relatively similar. The only key differences are the names of the package files that you will download and the commands you will use to install Chef.

The high-level steps you will take are as follows:

1. Downloading the Chef installer for your platform.
2. Installing the package as an administrative user.
3. Configuring the Chef service.
4. Testing the server using command-line tools.

Because steps 3 and 4 will be the same for both Ubuntu and Red Hat installation procedures, the instructions will be in a section following the Red Hat installation guide.

Installing on Ubuntu

The following are instructions for an Ubuntu-based system; they were performed on an Ubuntu 12.04 host, but should be identical for all supported Ubuntu distributions. For Red Hat-based installation instructions, see the next section.

Downloading the package

You can download the package by returning to the download page referenced previously (`http://www.getchef.com/chef/install/`), or you can download Version 11.0.10 directly from `https://opscode-omnibus-packages. s3.amazonaws.com/ubuntu/12.04/x86_64/chef-server_11.0.10-1. ubuntu.12.04_amd64.deb`.

Installing the package

In order to perform the installation, open a terminal on your Ubuntu host (either locally or connect via SSH) as a user who has administrative privileges. This can be done directly either as the root or any user who has permission to execute arbitrary commands via `sudo`.

Once you log in to the host, navigate to where you want to store the package (remember it's quite large, approximately 200 MB) and download the file using `curl`:

```
user@ubuntu:~ $ curl -O https://opscode-omnibus-packages.s3.amazonaws.
com/ubuntu/12.04/x86_64/chef-server_11.0.10-1.ubuntu.12.04_amd64.deb
```

Once the file is downloaded, the `dpkg` tool will be used to perform the package installation:

```
user@ubuntu:~ $ sudo dpkg -i chef-server_11.0.10-1.ubuntu.12.04_amd64.deb
```

Once this is finished, the Ubuntu-specific portion of the setup is complete, and you will need to configure Chef using the `chef-server-ctl` command, which we will discuss in the *Configuring Chef Server* section, following the *Installing on Red Hat Enterprise Linux* section.

Installing on Red Hat Enterprise Linux

Installation on a Red Hat Enterprise Linux distribution is as straightforward as installing any other package. You download the package to the local disk and install it using RPM tools.

Downloading the package

You can download the latest version of the package by returning to the download page referenced previously (`http://www.getchef.com/chef/install/`), or you can download Version 11.0.10 directly from `https://opscode-omnibus-packages. s3.amazonaws.com/el/6/x86_64/chef-server-11.0.10-1.el6.x86_64.rpm`.

In order to perform the installation, open a terminal on your Red Hat host (either locally or connect via SSH) as a user who has administrative privileges. This can be done directly either as the root or any user who has permission to execute arbitrary commands via `sudo`.

Once you log in to the host, navigate to where you want to store the package (remember it's quite large, approximately 200 MB) and download the file using `curl`:

```
user@rhel:~ $ curl -O https://opscode-omnibus-packages.s3.amazonaws.com/
el/6/x86_64/chef-server-11.0.10-1.el6.x86_64.rpm
```

How long this takes will vary according to the available bandwidth but should take somewhere between 5 and 20 minutes on a reasonably fast connection.

Once the file is downloaded, the `rpm` tool will be used to perform the package installation:

```
user@rhel:~ $ sudo rpm -ivh chef-server-11.0.10-1.el6.x86_64.rpm
```

Once this is finished, the Red Hat-specific portion of the setup is complete, and you will need to configure Chef using the `chef-server-ctl` command, which we will discuss in the following section.

Configuring a Chef server

Historically, installing Chef requires manual editing of configuration files, choosing RabbitMQ credentials, installing CouchDB, and a handful of other tasks. Now, with the omnibus installer, all of this is taken care of for you. If you have been following along, your system has the Chef server and all of its dependencies installed on the system in the `/opt/chef-server` directory.

Included with the installation of the package is a shell script, `chef-server-ctl` (located at `/opt/chef-server/bin`), which is responsible for configuring your newly installed Chef server. In order to configure your services, you will need to run it as `root` because the scripts will need to modify your system in ways that your regular account may not be able to. Initializing the configuration tool is as simple as issuing the following command:

```
sudo chef-server-ctl reconfigure
```

Running this script may take a few minutes, and it will produce a lot of output while it is doing its work. While it is running, let's take a few minutes to discuss how it works and what it is doing.

Understanding how chef-server-ctl works

Earlier in this chapter, you were briefly introduced to the `chef-solo` tool. You saw how it can be used to manage your local server using on-disk recipes and configuration data. The Chef team has leveraged this ability to do just that with the Chef server using `chef-solo` to bootstrap the server configuration. If you were to look at the code for the `/opt/chef-server/bin/chef-server-ctl` script, you would see that the last line in the script executes the following command:

/opt/chef-server/embedded/bin/omnibus-ctl chef-server /opt/chef-server/ embedded/service/omnibus-ctl $@

If you follow the trail and dig into the `omnibus-ctl` script, you will find that it is just a wrapper around the `omnibus-ctl` Ruby gem. Digging into the `omnibus-ctl` gem, you will see that in the end, the `reconfigure` command you pass on the command line is a Ruby method that makes the following call:

```
run_command("chef-solo -c #{base_path}/embedded/cookbooks/solo.rb -j
#{base_path}/embedded/cookbooks/dna.json")
```

This tells us that the Chef omnibus package uses `chef-solo` to configure itself—a pretty clever trick indeed! You can see just how powerful a tool `chef-solo` can be, being able to configure and reconfigure the Chef service.

What's happening on my server?

What you will probably notice right away is that a lot of text is being scrolled past in your terminal window. If you were to look at the contents, you would see that it shows you the actions that are being taken by `chef-solo` to provision your new services. As there is a lot of information going past (thousands of lines), here is a high-level overview of what is happening on your host:

1. A new user, `chef_server`, and its corresponding group are being provisioned.

2. Chef services are being set up, and startup scripts for upstart are being placed in the appropriate system directories. The Run scripts for Chef services are located at `/opt/chef-server/sv`.

3. Chef state directories are being created in `/var` including `/var/opt/chef-server` and `/var/log/chef-server`.

4. RabbitMQ is being configured to store data in `/var/opt/chef-server` and log the output to `/var/log/chef-server` as well as its startup scripts in `/opt/chef-server/sv/rabbitmq/run`.

5. PostgreSQL is being configured with its data in `/var/opt/chef-server/postgresql/data` along with a user, `opscode-pgsql`, to run the service. Some system-level changes to share memory sizes are being set via `sysctl` to make PostgreSQL work as well as persisted in `systctl.conf`.

6. Solr is being set up to work with the configuration and data rooted in `/var/opt/chef-server/chef-solr/`, with the run script being placed in `/opt/chef-server/sv/chef-solr/run`.

7. Chef-expander (the data-indexing service) is being configured for `/var/opt/chef-server/chef-expander` as its working directory with Solr and RabbitMQ endpoints on the localhost. The run script is located at `/opt/chef-server/sv/chef-expander/run`.

8. The Chef bookshelf metadata service is readied in `/var/opt/chef-server/bookshelf/` with its run script at `/opt/chef-server/sv/bookshelf/run`.

9. Erchef, the Erlang Chef service, is installed and pointed at the local Solr, RabbitMQ, bookshelf, and PostgreSQL services.

10. The system is then bootstrapped using the bootstrap recipe. This recipe verifies that the system is running (by checking that the `http://localhost:8000/_status` returns an HTTP 200 response) and installs the SSL certificate for the web-based UI in `/etc/chef-server/chef-webui.pem`.

11. The web-based UI configuration files are generated and placed in `/var/opt/chef-server/chef-server-webui/`.

12. A copy of `nginx` to host the web UI is placed in `/var/opt/chef-server/nginx`, and the initial self-signed SSL certificates as well as the static assets are installed in `/var/opt/chef-server/nginx/html`.

13. The Chef API testing framework, `chef-pedant`, is installed.

14. Finally, `/etc/chef-server/chef-server-running.json` is generated with the current configuration settings for your Chef services.

Clearly, there is a lot happening here; if you have any outstanding concerns about what is being done, be sure to read through the output. One of the great things about Chef is that the recipes are just a set of scripts that you can open and view the contents of, and the output shows you what is happening during the execution. Everything it does is transparent and manageable by you.

Verifying that the services are running

Once the configuration of your services is complete, you will want to validate that the required services are running. Again, the `chef-server-ctl` script will be used, but we will invoke the `status` subcommand instead of the `reconfigure` subcommand, as shown in the following code:

```
user@host:~ $ sudo chef-server-ctl status
run: bookshelf: (pid 3901) 3123s; run: log: (pid 3900) 3123s
run: chef-expander: (pid 3861) 3129s; run: log: (pid 3860) 3129s
run: chef-server-webui: (pid 4053) 3095s; run: log: (pid 4052) 3095s
run: chef-solr: (pid 3819) 3135s; run: log: (pid 3818) 3135s
run: erchef: (pid 4230) 3062s; run: log: (pid 3937) 3117s
run: nginx: (pid 4214) 3064s; run: log: (pid 4213) 3064s
run: postgresql: (pid 3729) 3146s; run: log: (pid 3728) 3146s
run: rabbitmq: (pid 3423) 3172s; run: log: (pid 3422) 3172s
```

The `status` subcommand will show you the process ID of each component, how long it has been running for, the PID of the logging process associated with that service, and how long the logging service has been running. For example, we can see that `chef-server-webui` has a PID of 4053 and has been running for close to an hour, and the logger has a PID of 4052, having been running for just as long as the service.

As you can see, the installation of Chef yields a number of components that will need to be up and running in order to successfully use Chef. You should have the following components running and listening on the following network ports:

Component	What to look for in the process list	Port(s)	Public?
Chef API server	`Erchef` and `nginx`	80, 443	Yes
Web management console	`chef-server-webui` and `nginx`	80, 443	Yes
Data indexer	`chef-expander`	N/A	N/A
Solr	`java` (running `start.jar` in the Chef directory)	8,983	No
PostgreSQL	`postmaster`	5,432	No
RabbitMQ	`beam.smp` running `rabbit`	5,672	No

Public components need to be made available to any clients, nodes, or end users that expect to use the Chef service over the network. Configuring your infrastructure to ensure that your services are available via the network is outside of the scope of this book as there are a near-infinite number of possible network configurations.

At a higher level, make sure that any firewall devices or packet-filtering systems are not preventing traffic from reaching these services if you see that they are running, but are having difficulties in connecting to them. If any of these services are not running, you will need to consult the logfiles generated by the service to determine what might be preventing them from starting up.

Validating that your service is working

In order to work with Chef, you will need a way to interact with it. Fortunately, Chef provides a suite of command-line utilities, which we will discuss at length as the book progresses. There is one primary tool, `knife`, that allows an administrator to interact with the service in the command line. The `knife` tool is run from a workstation and provides many commands to view, search, and modify data maintained by the Chef service. Once you have installed and verified that all the services are running, we can move on to setting up knife.

 You will see that the standard place to store your Chef configuration data is in `$HOME/.chef` (on a UNIX-like system.) This is not mandatory, and these files can be stored anywhere you like.

The `knife` tool communicates with the Chef server via HTTP and uses certificates for authentication between the workstation and the server. In order to get started with `knife`, we will need to do two things: gain access to the certificates that were generated during the installation of Chef and then use those credentials to set up a new user in the system.

In the following examples, we will be using the host that the Chef services were installed on as our workstation (where we will use `knife`). If you want to use a different host, you will need to get the required certificate (`.pem`) files to your local machine using `scp` or some other mechanism. By using the following commands, we can get the required authentication materials into our work directory:

```
mkdir $HOME/.chef
sudo cp /etc/chef-server/admin.pem $HOME/.chef
sudo cp /etc/chef-server/chef-validator.pem $HOME/.chef
sudo cp /etc/chef-server/chef-webui.pem $HOME/.chef
sudo chown -R $UID $HOME/.chef
```

Chef uses a signed header authentication for requests to the API, which means there must be a shared key that is present on both the client and the server. Chef-server will generate the chef-validator.pem file when it is configured. New nodes or clients use the chef-validator.pem file to sign the requests used to register themselves with the system.

Once you have these files copied into your Chef work directory, it is time to configure knife itself. Fortunately, knife has an interactive configuration mode that will walk you through the process of generating a configuration file. First, ensure that you are using your Chef gemset (if you are using RVM as we discussed earlier) and then run knife on your workstation (again, in this example, we are using our Chef service host for both purposes):

```
user@chef:~$ rvm use 1.9.3@chef
user@chef:~$ knife configure -i
```

When you run knife with the -i flag, you will be prompted by the following questions, which you can answer with the defaults for almost everything (non-default answers are in bold):

```
WARNING: No knife configuration file found
Where should I put the config file? [/home/user/.chef/knife.rb]
Please enter the chef server URL: [https://localhost:443]
Please enter a name for the new user: [user]
Please enter the existing admin name: [admin]
Please enter the location of the existing admin's private key: [/etc/
chef-server/admin.pem] ~/.chef/admin.pem
Please enter the validation clientname: [chef-validator]
Please enter the location of the validation key: [/etc/chef-server/chef-
validator.pem] ~/.chef/chef-validator.pem
Please enter the path to a chef repository (or leave blank):
Creating initial API user...

Please enter a password for the new user:
Created user [user]
Configuration file written to /home/user/.chef/knife.rb
user@chef:~$
```

As mentioned earlier, this does two things:

- First, it uses the validation key and client name specified at the prompts to contact the API service and register a new client (user) with the service
- Secondly, it generates a configuration file for `knife` that has the settings needed to connect to the service from now on

Since Chef and its components are written in Ruby, the resulting configuration file is a Ruby script, which contains some code that configures `knife` so that it knows what API server to connect to, which key files to use, what client name to use, and so on.

An inspection of the configuration file that was generated by the previous command will look like the following:

```
log_level                  :info
log_location               STDOUT
node_name                  'user'
client_key                 '/home/user/.chef/user.pem'
validation_client_name     'chef-validator'
validation_key             '/home/user/.chef/chef-validator.pem'
chef_server_url            'https://localhost:443'
syntax_check_cache_path    '/home/user/.chef/syntax_check_cache'
```

Because we are using the service host as our workstation, the Chef server URL points to the localhost. If your workstation were to be a different system such as your laptop, then this URL would be the IP or hostname of the host running the Chef service.

Ensuring that your knife configuration works

After setting up `knife`, we can use it to validate that it was configured correctly by querying the Chef server using some simple commands. The `knife` commands follow the format `knife <command> <subcommand>`, where `command` is either a client, configuration, cookbook, cookbook site, data bag, environment, exec, help, index, node, recipe, role, search, ssh, status, or tag. Subcommands will vary with the command, but they typically include things such as show, create, list, and delete (among others).

As there will initially be no nodes, cookbooks, recipes, roles, data bags, and such, we will query the list of clients that the server knows about. This should be a list of two clients: `chef-webui` (as it is a consumer of the API itself) and `chef-validator` (without it, it wouldn't be possible to register a new client).

The client command, with the list subcommand, prints a list of clients that the server knows about. At this point, running the command would look like this:

```
user@chef:~$ knife client list
chef-validator
chef-webui
user@chef:~$
```

 If you do not get the previous output, but get an error instead, you will need to go back and make sure that all the previous steps are completed and verified.

Once you know that it works, you can use knife to interact with the API. Unfortunately, we do not have much data in the system just yet, but we can use the show subcommand in conjunction with the client command and a client name to display more detailed information about a client:

```
user@chef:~$ knife client show chef-webui
admin:      true
chef_type:  client
json_class: Chef::ApiClient
name:       chef-webui
public_key: -----BEGIN PUBLIC KEY-----
MIIBIjANBgkqhkiG9w0BAQEFAAOCAQ8AMIIBCgKCAQEAos5cQ1NxP7zKf1zRM33g
YeVyHNOO5NcICjSIvqQ5A37wwLfgtPLJQqboW7ZcNL3xYcKOlfYSEK7xha3ss8tT
A+XMifaFp3JsdheyPeIJir2bc9iltUUcbpw9PJ2aQKTB1FNx23A7ag+zBfxcDjbY
7RkdcziwB74ynd6e/K8c0JTRnA5NxoHkFc6v8a/itwujGwugWJXDQunWfCmAvjws
JgDOUu2aHOCVIVkc8it51Sc7Anx0YnCjNmdhz1xIo0MOVNOEmC9ypP0Z7mVv1C69
WWBOEvS9zimjXo4rxBwFmWkPEIG6yPQjhuNmFd69K14vZQtAsH07AZFRSS7HLWnZ
WQIDAQAB
-----END PUBLIC KEY-----

validator:  false
user@chef:~$
```

Summary

Congratulations! If you have gotten this far, you now have a fully functional Chef service and a copy of the command-line utilities, including chef-solo. You now have covered the following:

- Using RVM
- Installing chef-solo
- Creating a simple recipe
- Running recipes with chef-solo
- Installing the Chef service
- Getting started with the `knife` utility
- Verifying that your Chef service is operating correctly

Now that you are able to use your Chef service, we can begin to investigate how to model our environment with Chef and see what it can do for us.

Modeling Your Infrastructure 2

Now that you have set up your server or are using the hosted offering, let's discuss how to model your infrastructure with Chef. Chef allows you to do this using building blocks that should be familiar to any system administrator.

This chapter will cover how to model your infrastructure with Chef. This will involve the following:

- Learning some terminologies and concepts relevant to Chef
- Analyzing a simple application infrastructure and seeing how it can be modeled with Chef
- Decomposing our architecture into the various components to be modeled
- Examining how data is stored and configurations are generated with Chef
- Bootstrapping and provisioning hosts with cloud providers such as AWS and Rackspace Cloud

Getting to know Chef

As with any other tool or system, there are new concepts and terminologies to be learned. Here are some terms that you may have seen or will see in this chapter:

- **Node**: A node is a system that is managed by Chef. These can be servers, desktop systems, routers, and anything else that is capable of running the Chef client and has a supported operating system.
- **Workstation**: A workstation is a special node that is used by a system administrator to interact with the Chef server and with nodes. This is where the command-line tools are executed, specifically the knife command-line tool.

- **Bootstrap**: This is a process of setting up a node to be used as a Chef client. This involves performing any work required to install the dependencies for Chef as well as Chef itself.

- **Bootstrap Script**: There are a number of possible ways to install Chef, Ruby, other core requirements, as well as any additional configuration that is needed for your specific systems. To provide this level of flexibility, the bootstrap process is scripted; on Windows, this is a batch file.

- **Recipe**: Recipes provide the instructions required to achieve a goal, such as installing a software package, configuring a firewall, provisioning users, installing printers, or managing other system resources. These are written in Ruby and executed on the nodes specified by the system administrator through the Chef console.

- **Cookbook**: A cookbook is a collection of recipes; typically, a cookbook provides one specific group of actions such as installing Apache or MySQL, providing Chef resources for a specific software tool, and so on.

- **Attributes**: Various components of the system have their own attributes and properties that describe how the software is to be configured. These properties are defined at various levels, ranging from node-specific settings to general defaults for a cookbook or a role.

- **Role**: A role is a collection of recipes and configuration data that describe how a resource should be configured in order to play that role in your overall system architecture. Examples of roles might include MSSQL Servers, Exchange Servers, IIS Servers, file servers, and so on. A role does not contain any knowledge of resources (systems) to apply the role to, only the configuration data.

- **Run List**: A run list is a list of recipes to be applied to a given node in a certain order. A run list can be composed of zero or more roles or recipes, and the order is important as the run list's items are executed in the order specified. Therefore, if one recipe is dependent upon the execution of another, you need to ensure that they run in the correct order.

- **Resource**: Resources are a way of describing what a recipe is performing. Some examples of resources would include files, directories, printers, users, packages, and so forth. A resource is an abstraction of something that is concretely implemented in a provider.

- **Provider**: A provider is a concrete implementation of a resource. For example, a user is a generic resource, but LDAP users or Active Directory users are concrete implementations of a user resource. The type of provider being selected will depend on some factors, such as the platform.

- **Data bags**: Data bags contain shared data about your infrastructure. Information that is not specific to a role or a resource, such as firewall rules and user accounts, will be stored in data bags. This is a good place to store system-wide configuration data.

- **Environments**: Environments provide a level of encapsulation for resources. For example, you may have two identical environments, one for testing and one for production. Each of these may have similar setups but different configurations, such as different IP addresses and users.

Modeling your infrastructure

Now that you're more familiar with some of the terms you need to know, let's take a look at a sample model and map it to Chef's components. At a higher level, the approach we will take is as follows:

1. Define an overview of your infrastructure that is decomposed into roles to be performed within the model (web servers, firewalls, database servers, and so on).

2. Collect or develop recipes that describe the configuration, software, and actions to be applied for those roles.

3. Bootstrap hosts with the Chef client so that they can participate in being managed.

4. Add any required configuration data into data bags to be used by nodes when running recipes such as IP address ranges, hostnames, users, software keys, or anything else that is specific to the active configuration.

5. Segregate hosts and configurations into different environments to provide a replicated infrastructure (development, staging, production, and so on). This step is optional.

In this chapter, we will be using Chef to build the infrastructure for a multi-tiered, photo-sharing application whose components are diagrammed in the following image:

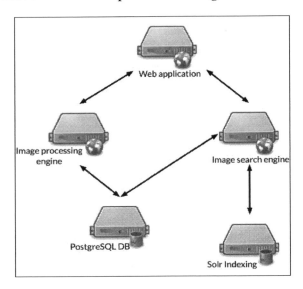

Building an architecture diagram gives us a good overview of our system so that we can have a map of the system before we start building it. It is important to note that a model of our infrastructure doesn't need to be mapped directly to resources (physical or virtual); rather, it provides an abstract, high-level overview of your systems. Once you have the model, you can apply it to the resources available as you see fit.

Our sample service-oriented web application is composed of the following software services:

- A frontend web application service
- An image-processing engine
- An image search engine

Each of these components is a **role** that is being played in the system. These roles may coexist on shared resources or may be applied to dedicated resources. A service-oriented architecture is a good example to work with for several reasons:

- It is flexible and scalable
- It will provide us with a complete system that is composed of multiple independent components to model, making it more interesting as an example

In this example, in addition to these roles, we might want to further configure our infrastructure to provide two different environments: one for staging and integration testing and one for production. Again, because this is a model, our staging environment and production environment will be composed of the same roles and have the same overall architecture; however, each will have different resources and configuration data associated with them. You may choose, for example, to consolidate resources in a test environment in order to keep costs down.

For this initial overview, we will assume that we have an account with a popular cloud-server-hosting company, that the network and operating systems are installed and operational, and that we have a functional and configured Chef service and workstation.

In our hypothetical system, each service can be mapped to a specific role in Chef. To model the infrastructure described, we will have a number of roles, one per element in our architecture. In this case, we will build one role for each service in our stack as they provide very specific features.

Roles

A role describes a part that a system plays in your infrastructure through a combination of recipes to execute and configure data. These roles can be fine-grained or broadly described, depending on your needs. There are benefits and drawbacks to both the approaches: fine-grained roles are smaller and easier to work with but require a larger number of roles to manage, whereas broadly scoped roles are less flexible and not as reusable.

For example, consider a typical LAMP (Linux, Apache, MySQL, and PHP) stack. The stack could be represented by three roles: an Apache web service with PHP, a MySQL database service, and an OpenSSH service for administration. Alternatively, you could define one role that describes the installation of the MySQL database service, the SSH service, and the Apache service.

Roles themselves know nothing about resources; instead, they are a description of how to configure a system in order to fill that role. The system administrator, via the chef console, assigns roles to the node(s) that they will be applied to. This may be a one-to-one, one-to-many, or many-to-one mapping, depending upon your capacity planning. At any time, an administrator can change the list of roles that are applied to a node, adding or removing them as needed. For example, you might decide to apply all your roles to one host today for cost savings, but scale them out in the future as your budget and needs grow.

Defining roles

Let's take a look at some roles we might define to model our SOA application on as described earlier in the chapter. Here, we will define fine-grained roles as they are easier to dissect and deploy onto separate nodes later. At a higher level, the following roles are what our services need to provide.

A web application service role

When defining what a web application server will need to do, we will need the following:

- nginx HTTP service
- Ruby 2.0
- Memcached service
- PostgreSQL client libraries
- Open TCP ports on the external networks: 80 for HTTP and 443 for HTTPS

An image-processing role

This role requires some image-processing libraries and custom software to be installed:

- ImageMagick libraries
- Git (to check out the source code)
- Build tools (to compile our source)
- The latest version of our image-processing software

An image search role

A service that provides image searching through perceptual hashing will provide an image search role functionality. This role will require the following:

- A Java runtime environment (JRE or JDK)
- Our custom-built service that is developed in Java
- TCP port 8999 open to internal hosts

A PostgreSQL service role

For the PostgreSQL database service role, the list is as follows:

- PostgreSQL 9.x server
- TCP port 5432 open to internal network clients
- Database backup software to back up data to an external cloud data storage service such as S3

A Solr service role

A system that provides the Apache Solr service will need the following:

- A compatible Java runtime (Oracle JRE or OpenJDK)
- TCP port 8993 open to internal servers
- Apache Solr itself

An OpenSSH service role

An OpenSSH service role will need the following:

- OpenSSH server
- TCP port 22 open on all the interfaces

Notice that these roles have no specific host information, such as IP addresses or servers to install the software on to; instead, they are blueprints for the packages we need to install and the configuration that those roles will provide, such as open ports. In order for these role definitions to be made as reusable as possible, we will write our recipes to use node- and role-specific configuration or data from our data bags to provide the required configuration data.

In order to define these roles, you will need recipes that describe the sets of steps and operations that will be applied to hosts in order to fulfill each role. For example, the PostgreSQL database server will require you to install PostgreSQL, open the firewall, and so on. These definitions are created by developing recipes that contain the necessary information to perform the tasks required, such as installing packages, generating configuration files, executing commands, and so on. Most of the services mentioned here (our custom imaging software being the likely exception) have cookbooks that already exist and are available for download.

Implementing a role

Now that you have seen what our infrastructure might look like at a higher level, let's take a look at how we will go about implementing one of our roles in Chef. Here, we will implement the PostgreSQL server role as it is simple to configure and has a very robust cookbook available already.

As mentioned before, you will need to either develop your own cookbooks or download existing ones in order to build your systems. Fortunately, there are thousands of cookbooks already written (over 1,500 as of this writing in the Chef Supermarket) and, as we will see in further chapters, developing new cookbooks is a straightforward process.

In order to define a role, we need to create it; this can be accomplished through a web interface or by using knife. Here, and elsewhere in this book, we will use knife as the way to interact with the Chef service because it provides a consistent experience across self-managed and hosted Chef. So let's get started!

The first thing you will need to do is create a new role with knife, which is as simple as executing the following:

```
knife role create -d postgresql_server
```

This will tell knife to connect to your Chef server's API and create a new role named postgresql_server. The -d flag tells knife to skip opening an editor and instead accept the default values. If you want to see what the underlying JSON looks like, omit the -d flag and make sure you have an appropriate EDITOR environment variable set. Once you run this, you can verify that your role was created with the following command:

```
knife role list
```

This will show you that you have a single role in the system, postgresql_server. Currently, however, this role is empty and has no information associated with it, just a name and an entry in the system. Now that we have a role in the system, let's look at how we can work with some recipes to make our role do something useful, such as install the PostgreSQL service.

Determining which recipes you need

Recipes are how Chef knows how to make sure that the correct packages are installed, what commands need to be executed in order to open ports on the firewall, which ports need to be opened, and so on. Like any good cook, Chef has a wide array of cookbooks at its disposal, each of which contains recipes relevant to that particular set of functionality. These cookbooks can either be developed by the system administrator or downloaded from a variety of places such as GitHub, BitBucket, or from a collection of cookbooks maintained by the Chef community on the Chef Supermarket (`http://supermarket.getchef.com`). We will discuss how to download and get started with some simple recipes and then further discuss how to develop and distribute our own recipes in later chapters.

Considering how we have arranged our roles, we would need recipes to install and configure the following:

- nginx
- A PostgreSQL server
- A PostgreSQL client
- Ruby 2.0
- Solr
- Java
- OpenSSH
- A Memcached server
- Memcached client libraries
- ImageMagick
- Git
- A Custom imaging software (we will call it **Image-O-Rama**)

Here, we will take an in-depth look at the recipe required for our PostgreSQL server and how we can leverage that to install the service on a host.

Installing a cookbook

Installing a cookbook for use on our clients is quite simple and involves only two steps:

1. Developing a cookbook, or downloading the cookbook from somewhere.
2. Uploading the cookbook to the Chef service using `knife`.

To get started, we will download an existing PostgreSQL cookbook from the Chef cookbook collection and upload it to our Chef service. Note that in order to install the PostgreSQL cookbook, you will also need to install any dependencies that are required. For simplicity, they are provided here as part of the instructions; however, you may find that when you experiment with other cookbooks in the future, you will need to download a few cookbooks before all of the dependencies are met, or use a tool such as Berkshelf for managing them.

To download a cookbook from Chef's provided collection of cookbooks, we will use knife with the following command:

```
knife cookbook site download <cookbook_name>
```

In this case, we will need to download five different cookbooks:

*   postgresql
*   build-essential
*   apt
*   chef-sugar
*   openssl

For each of the items in the list, we will download them using the following command:

```
knife cookbook site download postgresql
knife cookbook site download build-essential
knife cookbook site download apt
knife cookbook site download chef-sugar
knife cookbook site download openssl
```

Each download will result in an archive being downloaded to your workstation. These archives contain the cookbooks, and you will want to decompress them after downloading them. They can be downloaded anywhere, but it would probably be a good idea to keep them in a common cookbooks directory, something like `chef/cookbooks` inside your home directory would be a good idea if you need one.

Once they are downloaded and decompressed, you will need to upload them to the Chef service. This can be done with only one command using `knife cookbook upload` as follows; they are uploaded from the directory in which you stored your decompressed cookbooks:

```
knife cookbook upload -o . apt build-essential postgresql chef-sugar
openssl
```

This will upload the five cookbooks we downloaded and tell knife to search the current directory by way of the `-o` . directive. Once this is done you can verify that they have been installed using the `knife cookbook list` command.

Once they are installed, your cookbooks are registered with the Chef service, and we can take a look at how we can configure and apply the PostgreSQL server to a new Ubuntu host.

Applying recipes to roles

Now that you have some cookbooks registered with your Chef service, you need to add them to a role's run list in order for their behavior to take effect on any end hosts. The relationship between a recipe and any given node is shown in the following diagram:

Because of the nature of this relationship, recipes deliberately have no knowledge of individual nodes. Just as a recipe for chocolate chip cookies has no idea about who manufactured the rolling pin and spatula; a Chef recipe is simply a set of instructions on what to do and in what order to perform those actions.

Because we have uploaded our cookbooks to the system, we have already added the recipes contained inside of those cookbooks to our system; therefore, we can now associate a recipe with our recently created role. If you look at the contents of the recipes directory inside of the `postgresql` cookbook, you will see that there is a `server.rb` file. This describes a recipe to install the PostgreSQL server and is what we will be adding to our `postgresql_server` role in order to perform the actual installation.

To do this, we need to edit our role and add the recipe to its run list; we will do this using knife.

Ensure that you have a valid text editor in your EDITOR environment variable; otherwise, you will have difficulty editing your entities with knife.

In order to edit our role, we can use the knife role edit command:

```
knife role edit postgresql_server
```

This will open the JSON file that represents the postgresql_server role stored in the Chef server in a text editor where you should see the following content:

```
{
  "name": "postgresql_server",
  "description": "",
  "json_class": "Chef::Role",
  "default_attributes": {
  },
  "override_attributes": {
  },
  "chef_type": "role",
  "run_list": [

  ],
  "env_run_lists": {
  }
}
```

The most important section of this JSON blob at this moment is the run_list key—this is an array of all the things we want to run. This can be a list of recipes or roles, and each of those has the following naming structure:

- recipe[cookbook::recipe] for recipes
- role[role_name] for roles

So our server recipe inside our postgresql cookbook would therefore be named "recipe[postgresql::server]". This is exactly what we will be adding to our role's run list JSON. Update the run_list entry from the original value of an empty array:

```
"run_list": [

],
```

To include our PostgreSQL server recipe, use the following code:

```
"run_list": [
  "recipe[postgresql::server]"
],
```

This is all we need to change now in order to apply the PostgreSQL server role to our node.

 Notice that we have not added any values to the role's attributes; this means that our recipe will be executed using its default attributes. Most recipes are written with some set of acceptable default values, and the PostgreSQL server recipe is no different.

For now, there is no need to modify anything else, so save the JSON file and exit your editor. Doing this will trigger knife to upload your modified JSON in place of the previous JSON value (after doing some validation on your JSON contents), and the role will now have the `postgresql::server` recipe in its run list. You should see an output from knife indicating that the role was saved, and you can verify that this is the case with a simple knife role show command:

```
knife role show postgresql_server
```

This will show you an overview of the role in a more human-readable format than the source JSON. For example, our role should now have one entry in the run list as shown in the following output:

```
chef_type:              role
default_attributes:
description:
env_run_lists:
json_class:             Chef::Role
name:                   postgresql_server
override_attributes:
run_list:               recipe[postgresql::server]
```

Once this is complete, our role is now ready to be applied to one of our nodes. At this point, we have uploaded our cookbooks, defined a role, and associated a recipe with our newly created role. Now let's take a look at the final step: applying our new role to a node.

Mapping your roles to nodes

As has been discussed, roles are a definition of what components need to be brought together to serve a particular purpose; they are independent of the hardware they are applied to. This helps to separate concerns and build reusable components to accelerate the configuration of infrastructure in new arrangements. In order to manifest a role, it must have a node that the role is applied to; in order to manage a node, it must have the Chef client and its dependencies installed and be registered with the Chef service.

Once a node is registered with Chef, you can set node-specific properties, assign roles and run the `chef-client` tool on the host in order to execute the generated run lists. For our sample application stack, we may have the following hosts running Ubuntu Linux 14.04:

- cayenne
- watermelon
- kiwi

Once they are bootstrapped and registered with the Chef service, we will then decide which roles are to be applied to which nodes. This could yield a configuration that looks like the following:

- cayenne
  - Web application service role
- watermelon
  - A PostgreSQL database role
  - A Solr search engine role
- kiwi
  - An image-processing role
  - An image search role

Without any hardware, roles are just an abstract blueprint for what needs to be configured together to provide a particular type of functionality. Here, we have combined our resources (cloud instances or dedicated hardware) and our recipes to build a concrete instance of our services and software.

In order to apply our newly created role to our host, watermelon, we will need to bootstrap that host, which will install the Chef client on the host and then register it with the Chef service. This is really a simple process, as we will see here, and is achieved using the `knife bootstrap` command:

```
knife bootstrap -x root -d ubuntu14.04 <ip address>
```

 For our example, the node will use an Ubuntu 14.04 host created on DigitalOcean, an inexpensive cloud-hosting provider; you can bootstrap just about any modern Linux distribution, but if you are following along with the commands in the book, you will get the best results by using an Ubuntu 14.04 machine.

This process will go through the steps required to install the Chef client on the node and register it with your Chef service. Once it is complete, you will see that the Chef client has finished with an output similar to the following:

```
Chef Client finished, 0/0 resources updated in 4.264559367 seconds
```

If you want to verify that the host has been added, a simple `knife node list` command will show you that it has been registered with the Chef service. If you don't see the client output above, or you don't see the newly bootstrapped node in your list, make sure that the output of `knife` bootstrap doesn't indicate that anything went wrong along the way.

Once our node is registered, we can add our `postgresql_server` role to our node's run list using the following knife command:

```
knife node run_list set watermelon role[postgresql_server]
```

This command will set the run list on our new host, watermelon, to contain the `postgresql_server` role as its only entry. This can be verified using the `knife node show` command:

```
knife node show watermelon
```

```
Node Name:    watermelon
Environment:  _default
FQDN:         watermelon
IP:           162.243.132.34
Run List:     role[postgresql_server]
Roles:
Recipes:
Platform:     ubuntu 14.04
Tags:
```

Now that the node has a run list with entries, it's time to actually converge the node. Converging a node means that the Chef server will compile the configuration attributes and then provide the end host with a complete list of recipes to run along with the required cookbook data and then execute them on the node.

Converging a node

Converging a node is done by executing the `chef-client` command-line utility on the host; this can be done in one of two different ways. The simplest way is to SSH into the host using an SSH client and then execute `chef-client` as the root; another way is to use knife to execute a command on a set of hosts in parallel, which will be discussed in later chapters. For now, simply SSH into your server and run `chef-client` as the root:

```
root@watermelon:~# chef-client
```

The Chef client will connect to the Chef service and download any information needed to execute its complete run list. A node's run list is determined by expanding every entry in the node's run list until it is a list of recipes to execute. For example, our node contains one element in its run list, the `postgresql_server` role. This role, in turn, contains one entry, the `postgresql::server` recipe, which means that the fully expanded run list for our node contains only one entry. In this simple case, we could have just added the recipe directly to our node's run list. However, this has a number of shortcomings, including not being able to add extra configuration to all the PostgreSQL servers in our infrastructure, as well as a number of other reasons that will be discussed in the future.

In addition to computing the run list, the Chef service will also determine what the final set of configuration data for our node will look like and then deliver it to the client. This is computed according to a set of rules shown later in this chapter. Once that is delivered, the client will also download all the cookbooks needed in order to know how to execute the recipes specified in the final run list. In our case, it will download all the five cookbooks that we uploaded previously, and then, when the client run is complete, the result will be presented in a running PostgreSQL server.

Once the client run is complete, it will report on how long the run took and how many resources were modified. The output should look something like the following:

```
Chef Client finished, 8/10 resources updated in 61.524995797 seconds
```

Assuming that nothing went wrong, you should now have a fully functional PostgreSQL server deployed to your new host. This can be verified by looking at the process list for a PostgreSQL process:

```
root@watermelon:~# ps ax |grep post
11994 ?   S   0:00 /usr/lib/postgresql/9.3/bin/postgres -D
```

There you have it, with only one command; your node has now been provisioned as a PostgreSQL database server. Now let's take a look at how we can use some other features of Chef to model our infrastructure.

Environments

Beyond creating roles and having resources to apply them to, there are often requirements around grouping certain resources together to create a distinct **environment**. An example of this might include building a staging environment that functions exactly like a production environment for the purposes of preproduction testing and simulation. In these cases, we would have an identical set of roles but would very likely be applying them to a different set of nodes and configuration values. Chef achieves this separation through the environment primitive, which provides a way to group separate configurations and hosts together so that you can model similar, yet separate, portions of your infrastructure.

In our hypothetical infrastructure, the three hosts in our production environment may be condensed down to one server in preproduction in order to save money on resources (or for other reasons). To do this, we would need to bootstrap a node, perhaps named `passionfruit` and then configure it to have all of the roles applied to it, rather than spreading them out across systems, as shown in the following figure:

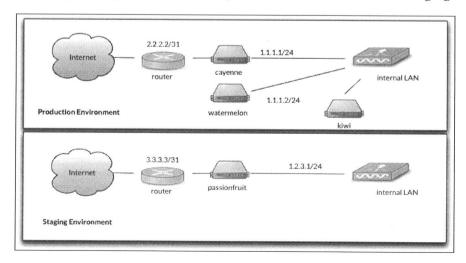

Here, in the previous image, you can see that each environment has a very similar setup but a different set of IP addresses and resources. Even though we have a heterogeneous hardware scale in our environments (production has three nodes, and preproduction has only one), any changes we make will be applied to all of the systems in a consistent manner.

In order to achieve this type of functionality, Chef needs a way to organize and compile the configuration data in order to provide it to the end host when the time comes to configure the host. Now that we understand how to model our systems with Chef, let's take a look at how Chef handles the configuration data to make all of this happen.

Organizing your configuration data

Chef runs on configuration data—this data can be stored in a variety of different locations, and with a variety of purposes. When computing the final configuration for a given node, the sources of configuration data are then "squashed" into a single, authoritative configuration to be deployed. Those sources include the following:

- **Cookbooks**: To provide reasonable defaults for recipes
- **Nodes**: Node-level overrides and defaults
- **Roles**: Per-role configuration data
- **Data bags**: System-wide configuration data storage

Data from these locations is combined to produce a final hash of attributes when a client requests its run list from the server. Cookbooks provide a baseline set of attributes that the recipes inside rely on. These attributes act as "sane defaults" for the recipes that, in the absence of overriding values, are sufficient to execute the recipes without extra work. Other sources, including the environment, role and node itself, may in turn override these attributes in order to provide the final configuration.

When developing recipes, these attributes can be accessed through the node hash and are computed by Chef using a set of rules to determine precedence. The order of precedence when computing this hash is broken down into the following levels (lowest to highest priority):

- Default
- Normal (also **set**)
- Override

Within each level, the sources of attribute data in order of increasing precedence are as follows:

- The attributes file inside of a cookbook
- Environment
- Role
- Node

This means that a node-specific override attribute takes precedence over all others, which in turn is more important than the role, environment and cookbook override attributes, and so down the chain of precedence. As your scope becomes narrowed from the most generic description of a role—the recipes—to the most specific component in the system—the actual node itself—these settings override the more generic values. A node knows best what the authoritative configuration should be as opposed to a recipe, which does not know anything about resources on the host. For example, consider the following scenario in which you have two hosts, *potassium* and *chromium*. For some legacy reason, their disks are configured slightly differently, as follows:

Potassium:

- 16 GB root partition
- 250 GB SSD data partition in /opt

Chromium:

- 32 GB root partition
- 400 GB EBS disk mounted at /usr

In order to install the PostgreSQL database server, you need to make sure you install it at a location that provides enough storage space for the data. In this example, there will be more data than either root disks can contain. As a result, the data directory will need to reside in /opt on potassium and /usr on chromium. There is no way that the PostgreSQL recipe can account for this, and the postgresql_server recipe does not know anything about its resources. Subsequently, the logical place to configure the data directory is at the node level. If the default location according to the recipe were /usr/local, then a node-level override may not be needed for chromium; however, in the case of potassium, it could be directed to store data in /opt/data instead.

What all this means is that as you develop recipes, any *default* attribute set by your cookbook will be the lowest priority. You can safely set some reasonable defaults in your cookbook knowing that they will only be used as a fallback if nobody overrides them further down the chain.

Example attribute data

A simple default attributes file for PostgreSQL cookbook might look like the following:

```
default['postgresql']['port'] = "5432"
default['postgresql']['data_dir'] = "/usr/local/pg/data"
default['postgresql']['bind_address'] = "127.0.0.1"
```

Notice that the attributes for a cookbook are a Ruby hash. Typically, good practice dictates that the namespace (first key in the hash) is the same name as the cookbook (in this case, postgresql), but this does not need to be the case. Due to cookbooks often containing multiple recipes, a cookbook's attributes file will often have per-recipe default configurations. Consider a further evolution of the PostgreSQL attributes file if it were to contain recipes for both the server and the client installation:

```
default[:postgresql][:client][:use_ssl] = true
default[:postgresql][:server][:port] = "5432"
default[:postgresql][:server][:log_dir] = "/var/log/pglog"
```

There are times when just a simple attributes file doesn't make sense because the configuration may be dependent on some property of the node being managed. The fact that the attributes file is just a Ruby script allows us to implement some logic inside our configuration (though you should avoid being overly clever). Consider a recipe where the default group for the root user depends on the platform you are using: "user d on BSDs, "n BSDs on Ubuntu Linux, and "n Ubu elsewhere. Chef provides a method, value_for_platform, that allows the attribute to be changed depending on the platform the recipe is being executed on, as the following example demonstrates:

```
default[:users][:root][:primary_group] = value_for_platform(
  :openbsd   => { :default => "wheel" },
  :freebsd   => { :default => "wheel" },
  :ubuntu    => { :default => "admin" },
  :default   => "root"
```

Where it makes sense, attributes can also be shared between cookbooks. There are limited uses for this, and it should be used with care as it blurs the boundaries between cookbooks and causes them to become too tightly coupled with one another.

Data bags

There are times when configuration data transcends a recipe, role, environment, or node. This type of configuration data tends to be system-wide data such as the following:

- Firewall rules for various types of hosts
- User accounts
- SSH keys
- IP address lists (white lists and black lists)
- API keys
- Site configuration data
- Anything that is not unique to a specific entity in your infrastructure

Data bags are very free-form, as the name implies; recipes that rely on data from data bags will impose their own expectations of the organization within a data bag, but Chef itself does not. Data bags can be considered, like all other Chef configuration data, to be one large hash of configuration data that is accessible to all the recipes across all the nodes in the system.

Knowing when to use data bags

Building firewall rules are a good use case for data bags. A good cookbook is an island by itself; it makes as few assumptions about the world as possible in order to be as flexible and useful as it can be. For example, the PostgreSQL cookbook should not concern itself with firewall rules, that is, the realm of a `firewall` cookbook. Instead, an administrator would leverage a generic firewall model and a cookbook with a specific firewall implementation such as the UFW cookbook to provide those features. In this case, if you were to look at the UFW cookbook, you would see the `ufw::databag` recipe making use of data bags to make the firewall rules as flexible as possible.

 UFW stands for uncomplicated firewall, a popular iptables-based firewall rule generation package for Linux that comes with many modern distributions and eases the management of a firewall configuration.

In this case, `ufw::databag` expects that there is a specific data bag named firewall and inside of it are items that share names with roles or nodes; this is in line with the notion that data bags are free-form, but certain cookbooks expect certain structure. If our infrastructure model had two roles, `web_server`, and `database_server`, then our firewall data bag would have contained two items named accordingly. The `web_server` item could look like the following hash:

```
{
  "id": "web_server",
  "rules": [{
    "HTTP": {
     "dest_port": "80",
     "protocol": "tcp"
    },
      "HTTPS": {
          "dest_port": "443",
          "protocol": "tcp"
      }
  }]
}
```

Here, `id` of the item maps to the name of the item, which is also the name of the role, so that the `ufw::databag` recipe knows where to fetch the data it needs to build its internal firewall rules. To compute its list of firewall rules to apply, the `ufw::databag` recipe examines the list of roles that the node is configured with and then loads the corresponding data from the items in the firewall data bag.

As you can see, data bags allow you to store centralized, free-form configuration data that does not necessarily pertain to a specific node, role, or recipe. By using data bags, cookbooks for configuring users, databases, firewalls, or just about any piece of software that needs shared data can benefit from the data stored in a data bag.

One might wonder why we have data bags when we already have attribute data, and that would be a good question to ask. Attributes represent the state of a node at a particular point in time, meaning that they are the result of a compaction of attribute data that is being supplied to a node at the time the client is being executed. When the Chef client runs, the attribute data for all the components contributing to the node's run list is evaluated at that time, flattened according to a specific priority chain, and then handed to the client. In contrast, data bags contain arbitrary data that has no attachment to a specific node, role, or cookbook; it is free-form data that can be used from anywhere for any purpose. One would not, for example, be likely to store user configuration data in a cookbook or on a specific node because that wouldn't make much sense; users exist across nodes, roles, and even environments. The same goes for other data such as network topology information, credentials, and other global data that would be shared across a fleet.

Large-scale infrastructure

One of the many benefits of Chef is the power to apply roles to nodes at scale. This means that once you define a set of roles and some supporting recipes, you can apply them to one host just as easily as any other. There are many organizations that manage very large infrastructure using Chef, including companies such as Facebook, Ancestry, and Riot Games. With Chef, configuring one hundred hosts is as straightforward as configuring one host. Being able to achieve scalability goals while remaining cost-effective is a critical part of running a technology business. To this end, Chef provides tools to automate the creation, provisioning, maintenance and termination of virtual hosts using the provided tools, which can help achieve both scalability and conservation of resources. The next chapter discusses how to use Chef to extend your infrastructure into the cloud.

Summary

Now that you've learned the key terminology that Chef uses and dissected an example infrastructure a bit, you can see the following:

- Infrastructure can be decomposed into the various roles that resources (nodes) play within that infrastructure

- A combination of recipes and configuration data provide us with roles that describe a part of our overall infrastructure

- Chef analyzes the roles applied to hardware resources (nodes) and generates a run list that is specific to the node that those roles are being applied to

- A run list is then combined with the cookbooks, recipes, templates, and configuration data to build a specific set of scripts that are executed on the node when the chef-client is run

- We can apply these methodologies of automated configuration to cloud servers and physical systems alike.

Now that you understand how Chef models interact, let's take a look at how we can get started with cloud services using Chef.

3
Integrating with the Cloud

Being able to configure new hosts automatically means that if you outgrow your existing resources, you can easily bring up new servers to increase your capacity with very little effort. The Chef command-line tool, `knife`, provides the ability to provision new hosts with cloud services automatically from the command line if configured correctly. This chapter introduces you to using Chef with two popular cloud platform providers: Amazon EC2 and Rackspace Cloud. Here, you will learn to use `knife` with both of these providers in order to perform the following:

- Provision new hosts according to your hardware needs
- Bootstrap the Chef client and register hosts with the Chef service
- List your existing capacity
- Terminate unneeded capacity

You will see that all of this can be done using the command-line tools provided without ever having to log in to the provider's web interface, and all of this within a few minutes of time.

Leveraging the cloud

Cloud computing providers such as Rackspace Cloud and Amazon EC2 provide on-demand computing power at the push of a button, a feature that has become immensely popular with developers and systems administrators alike. One of the most touted benefits of cloud computing is cost savings; however, these on-demand instances can become very expensive if they are left running. Often the capacity of time will be configured in order to handle large-scale events and then left online because of the time required to reconfigure the systems if they are needed again. As underutilized capacity ends up costing money rather than saving it, being able to reduce or expand the capacity quickly and easily will help you match your computing needs while saving both time and money.

This section specifically looks at two of the more popular cloud providers: Amazon EC2 and Rackspace Cloud; however, there are others, and the techniques described here will be broadly applicable to any other supported cloud provider.

Amazon EC2

Amazon EC2 is a very popular cloud-computing platform, and `knife` has support to manage EC2 instances from the command line through the `knife-ec2` plugin. The following steps demonstrate how you can work with EC2:

1. Install the EC2 `knife` plugin.
2. Set up your SSH keys for use with EC2.
3. Configure `knife` with your AWS credentials.
4. Find the desired AMI.
5. Provision a new host with `knife`.
6. Bootstrap the newly created host.
7. Configure the new host with a role.

Installing the EC2 knife plugin

As of Chef 0.10, the `ec2` subcommands have been moved from being built in `knife` to an external gem, `knife-ec2`. In order to use EC2 commands, you will need to install the gem, which can be done via the following command:

```
gem install knife-ec2
```

This will install all of the gem dependencies that the EC2 plugin requires.

> Some of the cloud provider plugins have conflicting dependencies, so it may be best to leverage a gem manager in order to isolate them. For example, using RVM or rbenv, you might create one Rubygem environment per provider so that you could switch back and forth with a simple command such as `rvm gemset use chef-ec2`.

Setting up EC2 authentication

In order to manage your EC2 hosts, you will need your EC2 key-pair properly registered with SSH and your AWS access keys set in your `knife` configuration file.

To do the first, make sure you have your EC2 SSH keys downloaded and registered with your SSH agent. One way to do this is to add the following to your SSH configuration file, typically, $HOME/.ssh/config:

```
Host *.amazonaws.com
  ForwardAgent yes
  CheckHostIP no
  StrictHostKeyChecking no
  UserKnownHostsFile=/dev/null
  IdentityFile ~/.ssh/ec2_keypair.pem
```

In order to configure your AWS keys, you will need to add some information to your knife.rb configuration file ($HOME/.chef/knife.rb):

```
knife[:aws_access_key_id] = "YOUR ACCESS KEY"
knife[:aws_secret_access_key] = "SECRET KEY"
```

These keys tell knife which AWS credentials to use when making API calls to perform actions such as provision new hosts and terminate instances. Without this, knife will be unable to make API calls to EC2. With these required changes made, let's look at how to create a new EC2 instance with knife.

Provisioning an instance

Initially, we will look at provisioning an instance using one of the Ubuntu AMIs. With knife, we can specify the AMI to use, the availability zone to target, and the size instance to be created. For example, to create an m1.large size in the us-east-1e availability zone with Ubuntu 12.04.3 LTS, we would need to use the AMI with ami-23447f4a as its identifier.

In order to determine the AMI ID, you will need to look it up at the following URL:

```
http://uec-images.ubuntu.com/
```

 Remember that when deciding which AMI to use, some of the EC2 instances will be 32 bit and some 64 bit; choose the appropriate AMI based on the instance type, region, and storage method you want to use.

The progress of provisioning can be seen using the following command:

```
$ knife ec2 server create -I ami-23447f4a -f m1.large -Z us-east-1e -N
<node name> -x ubuntu --sudo
```

The output from the previous command will show you the progress of the provisioning (this may take a minute or two, depending on the region, instance size, how long status checks take, and so on):

```
[user]% knife ec2 server create -I ami-23447f4a -f m1.large -S ec2-
keypair -Z us-east-1e -N <node name> -x ubuntu --sudo
Instance ID: i-0dfec92d
Flavor: m1.large
Image: ami-23447f4a
Region: us-east-1
Availability Zone: us-east-1e
Security Groups: default
Tags: Name: i-0dfec92d
SSH Key: ec2-keypair

Waiting for instance................
Public DNS Name: ec2-54-80-59-97.compute-1.amazonaws.com
Public IP Address: 54.80.59.97
Private DNS Name: ip-10-157-31-234.ec2.internal
Private IP Address: 10.157.31.234
```

Bootstrapping the instance

As you can see, `knife` will tell you the public IP and public DNS name of the new instance along with the instance ID, tags, and so forth. Once the instance is provisioned and is online, it will need to be bootstrapped. Remember that bootstrapping will install the Chef client and register the instance with the Chef service, which we can do in the same way we bootstrap any other host:

```
$ knife bootstrap <instance-public-ip-address> -N <node-name> -x ubuntu
--sudo
```

As EC2 provisions each instance with an `ubuntu` user that has `sudo` privileges, we provide the bootstrap command with `-x ubuntu` and `--sudo` to ensure we have the required privileges to perform the bootstrapping. Additionally, as you more than likely do not want the AWS-provided DNS name as the node name, the Chef node name is set through the `-N <node-name>` command line flag. Once the bootstrap step is finished, assuming that there are no errors, verify that your newly provisioned host is listed in your chef service:

```
$ knife node list
```

The output will contain your newly bootstrapped node ID, as specified by you in the command line or the DNS name, if you don't specify a node name. You have now provisioned a new EC2 instance and registered it with your Chef service with only two commands!

Terminating the instance

Once you are done with testing, you may not want to leave the EC2 instance running, as it will incur costs if it remains idle. To ensure this doesn't happen, perform the following four steps:

1. List your EC2 instances
2. Delete the server from EC2
3. Remove the server from Chef
4. Verify that the instance no longer exists in Chef or EC2

To list our EC2 instances, use the `server list` subcommand of the `ec2` command, which will list all of the EC2 instances in the specified region. If you do not specify a region, `us-east-1` is the default region. The full command to list EC2 servers is as follows:

```
$ knife ec2 server list
```

As an example, executing this command after provisioning the first host will show a table of one instance as follows:

```
Instance ID   Name        Public IP     Private IP
i-0dfec92d    i-0dfec92d  54.80.59.97   10.157.31.234
```

For most `knife` commands, you will need the instance ID so the previous table can be truncated to fit in print.

> Listing EC2 nodes will result in a table that contains all the currently provisioned EC2 instances in the region by means of the EC2 API, which is separate from the Chef service API. This means you will get a list of all the instances in EC2 whether or not they are registered with Chef. The full table will contain most of the information you can see on the EC2 control panel, including the public and private IP, flavor, AMI, SSH key, and so on.

Deleting an instance is just as easy as creating or listing them. Here, the `server delete` subcommand is invoked with the instance identifier to be terminated. This will use the EC2 API to issue a terminate command—this is not reversible and so the command will prompt you to ensure that you really did want to delete the instance:

```
[user]% knife ec2 server delete i-0dfec92d
Instance ID: i-0dfec92d
Flavor: m1.large
Image: ami-23447f4a
Region: us-east-1
Availability Zone: us-east-1e
Security Groups: default
SSH Key: ec2-keypair
Root Device Type: instance-store
Public DNS Name: ec2-54-80-59-97.compute-1.amazonaws.com
Public IP Address: 54.80.59.97
Private DNS Name: ip-10-157-31-234.ec2.internal
Private IP Address: 10.157.31.234
Do you really want to delete this server? (Y/N)
WARNING: Deleted server i-0dfec92d
WARNING: Corresponding node and client for the i-0dfec92d server
were not deleted and remain registered with the Chef Server
```

Removing the Chef node

At this point, the EC2 instance is being terminated and removed from your account. However, it is not removed from the Chef service that needs to be done separately with the `node delete` command. Here, the Chef node name is specified, not the instance identifier:

```
$ knife node delete my-first-ec2-instance
```

Verify that the node was removed from Chef using `node list`:

```
$ knife node list
```

The output should show you that your EC2 instance is no longer registered with Chef.

Rackspace Cloud

Rackspace Cloud is another popular cloud-computing provider that is well supported by Chef. Similar to EC2, there is a `knife` plugin for Rackspace Cloud:

```
gem install knife-rackspace
```

In the same way that AWS requires a set of credentials to interact with the API to create and terminate instances, Rackspace Cloud has its own configuration. However, the Rackspace Cloud API is a little simpler; you will need to provide `knife` with your Rackspace Cloud's username and API key. For those who do not already have their API key, it can be found in your Rackspace Cloud control panel. The appropriate configuration to add to your `knife.rb` file is as follows:

```
knife[:rackspace_api_username] = "Your Rackspace API username"
knife[:rackspace_api_key] = "Your Rackspace API Key"
```

This data can be hard coded into your configuration file, or since the `knife` configuration file is just Ruby, it can be generated by evaluating environment variables or looking at a local file. This is useful if you are submitting your `knife.rb` file into a source repository so that credentials are not leaked.

Provisioning an instance

Rackspace Cloud server provisioning is just as straightforward as it is with EC2. There is some variation in the command-line options passed to `knife` because of the way Rackspace provides images for systems. Instead of using the instance size and an AMI, you can specify the flavor of the system to provision (the node's CPU, memory, and disk allocation) and the operating system to image the instance with. In order to determine what flavors are available, the `knife-rackspace` plugin provides the `rackspace flavor list` subcommand:

```
$ knife rackspace flavor list --rackspace-region=IAD
```

As it is possible that there are different capacities in different regions, it is a good idea to check what is available in the region where you want to provision a node. This will result in a list of flavors and their specifications; as of now, some of the current offerings in IAD are as follows:

ID	Name	VCPUs	RAM	Disk
2	512MB Standard Instance	1	512	20 GB
3	1GB Standard Instance	1	1024	40 GB
4	2GB Standard Instance	2	2048	80 GB
performance1-1	1 GB Performance	1	1024	20 GB
performance1-2	2 GB Performance	2	2048	40 GB
performance2-120	120 GB Performance	32	122880	40 GB
performance2-15	15 GB Performance	4	15360	40 GB

In addition to knowing which flavor to provision, you need an image identifier (similar to an AMI) to apply to the new host. Again, this list may vary with region and possibly change over time so there is a command, rackspace image list, to list the various images:

```
$ knife rackspace image list --rackspace-region=IAD
```

The output here is quite long, so it has been sampled to show enough to be useful:

```
ID                                    Name
ba293687-4af0-4ccb-99e5-097d83f72dfe  Arch 2013.9
41e59c5f-530b-423c-86ec-13b23de49288  CentOS 6.5 (PVHVM)
857d7d36-34f3-409f-8435-693e8797be8b  Debian 7 (Wheezy)
896caae3-82f1-4b03-beaa-75fbdde27969  Fedora 18 (Spherical Cow)
fb624ffd-81c2-4217-8cd5-da32d32e85c4  FreeBSD 9.2
1705c794-5d7e-44d6-87da-596e3cf92144  Red Hat Enterprise Linux 6.5
df27d481-63a5-40ca-8920-3d132ed643d9  Ubuntu 13.10
d88188a5-1b02-4b37-8a91-7732e42348c1  Windows Server 2008 R2 SP1
```

As you can see, there are a number of Linux, BSD, and Windows distributions available to provision. In order to provision a new host, you will use the server create command, similar to the EC2 command. The following knife command will provision a 512 MB host with Ubuntu 13.10 in the IAD datacenter:

```
$ knife rackspace server create -I df27d481-63a5-40ca-8920-3d132ed643d9
-f 2 --rackspace-region=IAD
```

As soon as the API responds to the request to provision a new host, you will see the Rackspace metadata for the host, such as the instance ID, name, flavor, and image:

```
Instance ID: 993d369f-b877-4f0f-be4b-cfc45c240654
Name: rs-21230044929009695
Flavor: 512MB Standard Instance
Image: Ubuntu 13.10 (Saucy Salamander)
```

Shortly after this—once the system has been provisioned, the network interfaces have been configured, and the root password has been set—the IP and root password will be displayed:

```
Public DNS Name: 162.209.104.248.rs-cloud.xip.io
Public IP Address: 162.209.104.248
Private IP Address: 10.176.65.92
Password: yZ3D3Tck8uGm
```

After SSH becomes available, `knife` will initiate the process of bootstrapping the host. By default, `knife` will use the `chef-full` template, which will install Chef via the omnibus installer for the platform you are bootstrapping. This can be altered by providing `knife` with the `-d` command-line option. Assuming that the host is bootstrapped properly, the system data will be displayed once again for your information:

```
Instance ID: 993d369f-b877-4f0f-be4b-cfc45c240654

Host ID: c478865ebb70032120024a9a2c8c65b9bb0913087991d4bab5acde00

Name: rs-21230044929009695

Flavor: 512MB Standard Instance

Image: Ubuntu 13.10 (Saucy Salamander)

Public DNS Name: 162.209.104.248.rs-cloud.xip.io

Public IP Address: 162.209.104.248

Private IP Address: 10.176.65.92

Password: yZ3D3Tck8uGm

Environment: _default
```

Once the bootstrap step is finished, assuming that there are no errors, verify that your newly provisioned host is listed in your chef service:

```
$ knife node list
```

The output will contain your newly bootstrapped node ID as specified by you in the command line (via `-N`) or the name generated by Rackspace (in this example, it will be `rs-21230044929009695`). Congratulations! You have provisioned a new Rackspace instance with a single command.

Terminating an instance

Once you are done with testing, you may not want to leave the EC2 instance running, as it will incur costs if it remains idle. To ensure this doesn't happen, perform the following four steps:

1. List your Rackspace servers.
2. Delete the server from Rackspace.
3. Remove the server from Chef.
4. Verify that the instance no longer exists in Chef or Rackspace.

To list your Rackspace instances, use the `server list` subcommand of the `rackspace` command, which will list all of the Rackspace instances in the specified region. Similar to the output from the EC2 server list command, the output will look like the following:

```
$ knife rackspace server list --rackspace-region=IAD


Instance ID                                  Name
993d369f-b877-4f0f-be4b-cfc45c240654   rs-21230044929009695
```

 Similar to the EC2 output, the resulting table is too wide for print so only the instance ID and node name is shown. You should expect to see public and private IP addresses, instance types, and some other data that you will be able to see on the Rackspace Cloud control panel as well.

You can delete an instance using a single command; the `server delete` subcommand is invoked with the Rackspace instance identifier to be terminated. Remember that this is not reversible, so the command will prompt you to ensure that you really do want to delete the instance:

```
$ knife rackspace server delete 993d369f-b877-4f0f-be4b-cfc45c240654
--rackspace-region=IAD


Instance ID: 993d369f-b877-4f0f-be4b-cfc45c240654
Host ID: c478865ebb70032120024a9a2c8c65b9bb0913087991d4bab5acde00
Name: rs-21230044929009695
Flavor: 512MB Standard Instance
Image: Ubuntu 13.10 (Saucy Salamander)
Public IP Address: 162.209.104.248
Private IP Address: 10.176.65.92


Do you really want to delete this server? (Y/N) y
WARNING: Deleted server 993d369f-b877-4f0f-be4b-cfc45c240654
WARNING: Corresponding node and client for the 993d369f-b877-4f0f-be4b-
cfc45c240654 server were not deleted and remain registered with the Chef
Server
```

Removing the Chef node

At this point, the EC2 instance is being terminated and removed from your account. However, it is not removed from the Chef service; this needs to be done separately with the `node delete` command. Here, the Chef node name is specified, not the instance identifier:

```
$ knife node delete rs-21230044929009695
```

```
Verify that the node was removed from Chef with node list:
```

```
$ knife node list
```

The output should show you that your recently created Rackspace instance is no longer registered with Chef.

Summary

The ability to scale your infrastructure through a combination of on- and off-site hosts is incredibly powerful. If you need more capacity, you can easily bring up new hosts on EC2, Rackspace Cloud, or any similar platform. Additionally, these techniques apply to not only public cloud providers but also to private cloud platforms such as VMWare vSphere and others (provided, a suitable plugin for `knife` exists).

As you have seen, with Chef you can spin up and spin down the server capacity to meet your needs with very little effort. Once your infrastructure management is automated, you can focus on higher level problems such as building scalable services and scaling to meet your customers' demands.

Expanding on this capability, you could use these tools to perform the following:

- Manually increase or decrease the capacity in order to match the demand
- Write a tool to analyze the current resource load and react accordingly
- Predict the future capacity and scale appropriately on a given schedule

Now that we have the ability to bring up some hosts to work with, we can take a look at how to work with cookbooks to learn how they work and how to build new ones.

4

Working with Cookbooks

Cookbooks are one of the fundamental components of the Chef system. They are containers for recipes, providers, resources, templates, and all the logic and information required to manage your infrastructure. This chapter covers the following:

- Organization of cookbooks
- Building cookbooks
- Developing recipes
- Handling multiple platforms for a cookbook organization

Cookbooks are one of the core components of Chef. They are, as their name suggests, a collection of recipes and other data that when combined provide a specific set of functionality to a system administrator. In each cookbook, you will find a collection of directories and files that describe the cookbook and its recipes and functionality. The core components of a cookbook are as follows:

- Cookbook metadata
- Attributes
- Recipes
- Templates
- Definitions
- Resources
- Providers
- Ruby libraries
- Support files

A cookbook is a collection of files and directories with a well-known structure. Not every cookbook has all of these components. For example, there may be no need to develop custom resources or providers in a cookbook that only uses Chef-supplied resources. However, every cookbook does need to have a metadata file that provides various bits of information such as its name, version, dependencies, and supported systems.

Let's take a look at the memcached cookbook as it is a reasonably simple cookbook that is capable of installing and configuring the memcache server, which is a distributed memory-backed cache service:

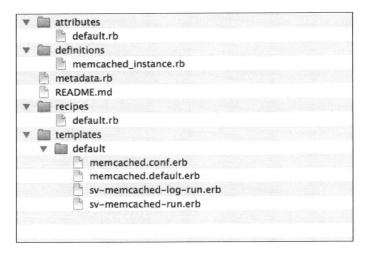

Here, you can see that this cookbook contains **attributes, definitions, recipes**, and **templates**, as well as a file named metadata.rb (the metadata file) and a README.md file. It is a good idea to provide examples of how to use your cookbook and recipes in some sort of documentation, such as a README.md file. When you look at the preceding screenshot, you will see that the directory names map to the component names and each contains some files or subdirectories with files. We will discuss the organization of the specific Chef components in greater detail further on as we dive into more details on each type later. For now, it is sufficient to know that the directory structure is designed to group together files for each type of component. Also notice that, as mentioned earlier, this cookbook is an example of one that does not have all the components, as there are no new **resources** or **providers** in this cookbook.

Some of these files are purely informational and have no effect on your recipes or Chef itself, such as the README.md file. This file, and others such as CHANGELOG, LICENSE, or DEVELOPMENT files, is included to convey information to you about how to participate, license, or otherwise use the cookbook.

There is a lot of information that is stored inside a cookbook—this information includes the steps to take in order to achieve a desired effect such as the installation of a service or provisioning of users on a host. A high-level overview of the content that we will be learning about in this chapter, so that you have an idea of how the components work together before you learn about them in depth, is shown as follows:

- **Attributes**: These are attributes that the cookbook's recipes rely on. A well-defined cookbook should contain some sane defaults for the recipes such as installation directories, usernames, downloadable URLs, and version numbers. Anything a recipe expects the node to have defined should be given a default value so that the recipe will behave as expected.

- **Recipes**: Ruby scripts define the recipes in the cookbook. A cookbook can contain as few as one or as many recipes as its author would like to put into it. Most package-specific cookbooks only contain a few recipes, while some cookbooks, such as your organization's private cookbook, may have dozens of recipes for internal use.

- **Templates**: These are Ruby ERB files that are used to describe any file that needs to have some dynamic data in it; often, these are used for startup scripts or configuration files.

- **Resources**: These describe a resource that can be used in a recipe. Resources are Ruby scripts that use Chef's resource **domain-specific language (DSL)** to describe various actions, attributes, and other properties of the resource.

- **Providers**: These describe an implementation of a resource; in the case of the supervisord cookbook, the service provider file outlines the actual implementation-specific logic of the actions that a resource can perform. There are many types of services that you could have: supervisord, runit, monit, bluepill, and so on.

Additionally, cookbooks may include a variety of support files that are not directly part of the recipes, such as the following:

- **Definitions**: These are used to build reusable templates for resources. Perhaps you want to define the structure of a user account, a background worker, or a runnable process. These are a way to programmatically describe what these look like and implement any logic they might need.

- **Ruby libraries**: Any reusable code that your recipes need can be included in the cookbook. Things that go in here are accessible by your recipes and automatically loaded for you.

- **Support Files**: These are arbitrary data files that don't fall into any of the other categories.

- **Tests**: Recipes, composed of Ruby code, can include unit tests or cucumber tests to verify that the logic works. Note that these tests are unit tests, not integration tests; they are not designed to ensure that you have configured your nodes properly or that there are no conflicts or other issues when applying these recipes.

Attributes

Attributes are Chef's way of storing configuration data and can be thought of as a large, but disjointed, hash structure. Chef pulls data from various locations and combines that data in a specific order to produce the final hash of attributes. This data is computed when a client requests its run list from the server (such as when you execute `chef-client` on a node). This mechanism allows you to describe data with a higher level of specificity at each step of the process, decreasing in scope going from the cookbook attributes files down to node-specific configuration data.

For example, imagine you are deploying PostgreSQL onto the hosts in your infrastructure. With PostgreSQL, there are a very large number of configuration options that can be tuned, ranging from open ports and number of concurrent connections down to memory used for key caches and other fine-grained configuration options. The cookbook's attributes files should provide enough configurations for PostgreSQL to work without making any modification to a host and without other things being deployed; also, they would most likely contain a pretty vanilla set of configuration values, which at a high level might look like the following:

- Install Version 9.3 from the source code
- Listen on Port 5432 on IP 0.0.0.0/0
- Store data in `/var/lib/postgresql`
- Create and use a `pgsql` user

Attribute data has not only a number of sources that it can be pulled from but also a set of priorities: default, normal, and override (in increasing order). Within each level, data is pulled from the cookbook attributes files and then from the environment, role, and node configuration data stored in the Chef server (in that order). Combined, this provides a comprehensive mechanism to define and customize the behavior of your recipes as they are applied to the nodes.

Now, as you can imagine, this is fine for a number of installations where the server has all of the space allocated on the root mount point, or doesn't have security restrictions about which IP addresses should be listened on, and so on. It would be nice to be able to say that in production, we want to use Version 9.3, but in a test environment, we want to install Version 9.4 in order to perform some tests that we don't want to run in production. We may also want to specify that in production, our hosts are EC2 instances with a customized EBS RAID for our PostgreSQL data and so the data should be stored in `/vol/ebs00/postgresql`. Using this multilayered approach for configuration data, this is entirely possible.

Attribute files contain Ruby code that stores the configuration data. In this case, to achieve our described default behavior, we could have a file, `attributes/default.rb`, that contains the following text:

```
default['postgresql']['port'] = "5432"
default['postgresql']['listen_address'] = "*"
default['postgresql']['data_dir'] = "/var/lib/postgresql"
default['postgresql']['install_method'] = "source"
default['postgresql']['version'] = "9.3"
```

The hash that this describes will look like the following JSON dictionary:

```
'node' : {
  'postgresql': {
    'port': '5432',
    'listen_address': '*',
    'data_dir': '/var/lib/postgresql',
    'install_method': 'source',
    'version': '9.3'
  }
}
```

Now, as described, we want to override the version in our staging environment to install Version 9.4; this means that in our staging environment, the configuration (exactly how to make this change will be discussed later) will need to have the following information:

```
'node' : {
  'postgresql': {
    'version': '9.4',
  }
}
```

When the Chef client runs on a node in the staging environment, the Chef server knows that the node is in the staging environment and will take the stage configuration above and overlay it on top of the defaults specified in the cookbook. As a result, the final configuration dictionary will look like the following:

```
'node' : {
  'postgresql': {
    'port': '5432',
    'listen_address': '*',
    'data_dir': '/var/lib/postgresql',
    'install_method': 'source',
    'version': '9.4'
  }
}
```

Notice that the version has been changed, but everything else remains the same. In this way, we can build very specific configurations for our hosts that pull information from a variety of places.

It is important to note that because these are interpreted Ruby scripts, their contents can range from simple attribute-setting statements to complex logic used to determine an appropriate set of default attributes. However, it's worth remembering that the more complicated your configuration is, the harder it may be to understand.

Multiple attribute files

Chef loads attribute files in alphabetical order and cookbooks typically contain only one attribute file named default.rb. In some cases, it makes sense to separate some of the attributes into separate files, particularly when there are a lot of them. As an example, the community-maintained MySQL cookbook has two attribute files: server.rb for the server attributes and client.rb with client-specific attributes. Each file contains anywhere between 50 and 150 lines of Ruby code, so it makes sense to keep them separate and focused.

Supporting multiple platforms

There are times when a simple attributes file doesn't make sense, so being able to dynamically define the defaults is very useful. Consider a multiplatform cookbook that needs to know which group the root user is in. The name of the group will vary according to the operating system of the end host. If you are provisioning a FreeBSD or OpenBSD host, then the group for the root will be `wheel`, but on an Ubuntu machine, the group is named `admin`. The attributes file can use plain old Ruby code or optional Chef-provided convenience methods such as `value_for_platform`, which is a glorified but compact switch statement:

```
default[:users]['root'][:group] = value_for_platform(
  "openbsd"   => { "default" => "wheel" },
  "freebsd"   => { "default" => "wheel" },
  "ubuntu"    => { "default" => "admin" },
  "default"   => "root"
)
```

Loading external attributes

Sometimes it is useful to load attributes from another cookbook; if your cookbook is tightly coupled to another cookbook or provides some extended functionality, it may make sense to use them. This can be achieved in the attributes file by using the `include_attribute` method (again, this is a Chef-specific convenience method).

Let's consider that you want to know the port that Apache is configured to use. You could use the `port` key from the `apache` configuration section, but it is not guaranteed that it exists (it may not have been defined or the recipe that contains it may not have been loaded yet). To address this, the following code would load the settings from `attributes/default.rb` inside of the `apache` cookbook:

```
include_attribute "apache"
default['mywebapp']['port'] = node['apache']['port']
```

If you need to load an attributes file other than `default.rb`, say `client.rb`, inside the `postgresql` cookbook, you can specify it in the following manner:

```
include_attribute "postgresql::client"
```

Make sure that any cookbooks you rely on are listed as a dependency in your cookbook's metadata. Without this, the Chef server will have no way of knowing that your recipes or configuration data depend on that cookbook, and so your configuration may fail as a result of this.

Using attributes

Once you have defined your attributes, they are accessible in our recipes using the **node hash**. Chef will compute the attributes in the order discussed and produce one large hash, which you will have access to.

 Chef uses a special type of hash, called a **Mash**. Mashes are hashes with what is known as indifferent access—string keys and symbol keys are treated as the same, so node[:key] is the same as node["key"]).

If we had the PostgreSQL attributes and user attributes as specified previously, without any overrides, then the resulting configuration will look like the following:

```
'node' : {
  'postgresql': {
    'port': '5432',
    'listen_address': '*',
    'data_dir': '/var/lib/postgresql',
    'install_method': 'source',
    'version': '9.3'
  },
  'users' : {
    'root' : { 'group' => 'wheel' },
  }

}
```

This data could then be accessed anywhere in our recipes or templates through variables such as node[:postgresql][port] or node[:users][:root][:group]. Remember that the final version of the node's configuration data is determined at the time the client makes the request for its configuration. This means that Chef generates a snapshot of the current state of the system, collapsed according to its rules of precedence, for that node and passes it to the host to perform its operations.

Metadata

Each cookbook contains a `metadata.rb` file in the root directory of the cookbook that contains information about the cookbook itself, such as who maintains it, the license, version, contained recipes, supported platforms, and the cookbook's dependencies. The contents of this script are used to generate a JSON file that describes the cookbook, which is used by the Chef server for dependency resolution, searching and importing into run lists.

This is a required file for a cookbook, and here is an example `metadata.rb` file from the PostgreSQL database server, which is slightly modified to fit the following:

```
name                "postgresql"
maintainer          "Opscode, Inc."
maintainer_email    "cookbooks@opscode.com"
license             "Apache 2.0"
description         "Installs and configures PostgreSQL"
long_description    IO.read(File.join(
                        File.dirname(__FILE__), 'README.md'
                    ))
version             "3.3.4"
recipe              "postgresql", "Includes postgresql::client"
recipe              "postgresql::ruby", "Installs Ruby bindings"
recipe              "postgresql::client",
                    "Installs client package(s)"
recipe              "postgresql::server", "Installs server packages"
recipe              "postgresql::server_redhat",
                    "Installs RedHat server packages"
recipe              "postgresql::server_debian",
                    "Installs Debian server packages"

%w{ubuntu debian fedora suse amazon}.each do |os|
  supports os
end

%w{redhat centos scientific oracle}.each do |el|
  supports el, ">= 6.0"
end

depends "apt"
depends "build-essential"
depends "openssl"
```

Because the `metadata.rb` file is a Ruby script, it allows you to use arbitrary Ruby code inside of it. Here, for example, the `long_description` entry is generated programmatically by reading in the contents of the supplied `README.md` file:

```
long_description  IO.read(File.join(File.dirname(__FILE__),
'README.md'))
```

Here, the PostgreSQL cookbook supports multiple platforms, so instead of writing each platform that is supported on a line of its own, you could use a loop similar to the one used in the `metadata.rb` file:

```
%w{ubuntu debian fedora suse amazon}.each do |os|
  supports os
end
```

Additionally, if it only supports certain platforms with a minimum version, you could write something similar to the following, which declares support for RedHat-based distributions greater than (or equal to) Version 6.0:

```
%w{redhat centos scientific oracle}.each do |el|
  supports el, ">= 6.0"
end
```

In this cookbook, the dependencies are listed line by line but could be represented similarly if you have a large number:

```
depends "apt"
depends "build-essential"
depends "openssl"
```

Dependencies could also be rewritten as follows:

```
%w{apt build-essential openssl}.each do |dep|
  depends dep
end
```

Obviously, in this case, you aren't saving any room; however, if you had ten or more dependencies, it could make it more compact.

As long as your Ruby code produces something that is a compatible argument or configuration, you can be as clever as you want. Take advantage of your ability to dynamically generate a configuration.

Recipes

Recipes are the core component of getting things done. They are scripts, written in Ruby, that provide the instructions to be executed on end hosts when the Chef client is run. Recipes are placed in the `recipes` directory inside of a cookbook, and each recipe is designed to achieve a specific purpose, such as provisioning accounts, installing and configuring a database server, and custom software deployments.

Recipes combine configuration data with the current state of the host to execute commands that will cause the system to enter a new state. For example, a PostgreSQL database server recipe would have the goal of installing and starting a PostgreSQL server on any host that runs the recipe. Let's look at a few possible starting states and the expected behavior:

- A host without PostgreSQL installed would begin at the state of not having the service; then, it will execute the commands required to install and configure the service

- Hosts with an existing but outdated PostgreSQL service would be upgraded to the latest version of the database server

- Hosts with a current installation of PostgreSQL would have its PostgreSQL installation untouched

- In all cases, the configuration on the disk would be updated to match the configuration stored in the Chef server

To achieve these goals, recipes use a combination of resources, configuration data, and Ruby code to determine what to execute on the end host. Each host-level resource — files, configuration files, packages, users, and so on — is mapped to a Chef resource in a recipe. For example, consider the recipe that we saw earlier in the book that was used to demonstrate that the Chef-solo installation was functional:

```
file "#{ENV['HOME']}/example.txt" do
  action :create
  content "Greetings #{ENV['USER']}!"
end
```

This is a complete recipe; it has one step to create a file, and that is all it does. The file being created on the end host needs a name; here, it will be named `ENV['HOME']/example.txt`, which is Ruby's way of representing `$HOME/example.txt`. In addition to a name, we are instructing Chef to create the file (we could just as easily instruct Chef to delete the file) and to put the contents *Greetings $USER* into the file, replacing what is in there.

We could extend our recipe to ensure that a specific user existed on the host and create a file with the owner set to the newly created user:

```
user "smith" do
  action :create
  system true
  comment "Agent Smith"
  uid  1000
  gid  "agents"
  home "/home/matrix"
  shell "/bin/zsh"
end

file "/tmp/agent.txt" do
  action :create
  content "Hello from smith!"
  owner "smith"
  group "agents"
  mode "0660"
end
```

Each recipe is a script that is run from beginning to end, assuming that nothing causes it to abort. Also, each recipe can access the node's attribute data and leverage resources to compile templates, create directories, install packages, execute commands, download files, and do just about anything that you can do from a shell as an administrator. If you can't accomplish what you need to do using the existing Chef resources, you can either create your own custom resources, or you can execute an arbitrary user-defined shell script.

Resources

Resources are programmatic building blocks in Chef; they are a declarative mechanism to manipulate a resource on a host. Resources deliberately hide the underlying implementation that is left to a provider. It is important to recognize that a resource describes what is being manipulated, not how it is being manipulated; this is by design, as it provides a high level of abstraction for Chef recipes to be as platform-neutral as possible.

For example, Chef has built-in resources that include the following:

- Cron jobs
- Deployments
- File system components (mount points, files and directories, and so on)

- Source code repositories (Git and svn)
- Logs
- PowerShell scripts (Windows targets)
- Shell scripts
- Templates
- Packages
- Users and groups

Resources combined with providers (discussed shortly) are collectively referred to as LWRPs or lightweight resource providers; they make up a large portion of the functionality within a Chef recipe.

Resources are composed of a resource name (package name, file path, service name, and so on), an action, and some attributes that describe that resource.

Using resources

Resources, as we have seen in some examples, take the following form:

```
resource_name <name parameter> <ruby_block>
```

In the preceding code, `resource_name` is the registered name of the resource, such as `file`, `package`, and `user`. The name parameter is a special argument to the resource that gives this resource a unique name. This is often also used by the resource as a default value for an attribute that naturally maps to the name of the resource such as filename, username, and package name (you can see a pattern here); however, you can use an arbitrary name attribute and manually set the attribute. The Ruby block is just a block of code in Ruby; this is how Chef's DSL works. In Chef, each resource expects some specific things inside its configuration block. You will find that many resources have different expectations, but in general, a resource block in a recipe will be of the following form:

```
resource_name "name attribute" do
    attribute "value"
    attribute "value"
end
```

The previous example, which created a new user, was the following:

```
user "smith" do
  action :create
  system true
  comment "Agent Smith"
```

```
    uid  1000
    gid  "agents"
    home "/home/matrix"
    shell "/bin/zsh"
  end
```

Here, the resource name is `user`, the name attribute is `smith`, and the block of code being passed to the resource has seven attributes: `action`, `system`, `comment`, `uid`, `gid`, `home`, and `shell`. Each of these attributes has a value associated with it; internally, the Ruby code for the resource will store these in some variables to be used when manipulating the specified resource. In this case, constructing a user on the end host through the correct provider will be helpful.

One of these attributes, `action`, is a bit unique; its job is to tell the resource what action to take on the resource. The list of available actions will be different with each resource, but typically, a resource will have actions such as create, delete, or update. Have a look at the documentation for the resource you are working with; the documentation will describe the available actions and what they do separately from the other attributes.

To demonstrate how the name attribute is used as a default value for the `user` resource, the following recipe has the same behavior as the previous one, but has one minor change:

```
user "agent_smith" do
  username "smith"
  action :create
  system true
  comment "Agent Smith"
  uid  1000
  gid  "agents"
  home "/home/matrix"
  shell "/bin/zsh"
end
```

Here, you can see that an additional attribute, `username`, has been added to the resource block with the value that was previously in the name attribute. Additionally, the name attribute has been changed to `"agent_smith"`. If you were to execute this recipe or the previous example, it would have the same effect: to create a local system user, `smith`, with the UID, GID, home, and other attributes specified.

Overriding a default behavior

In addition to properties, resources also have a default **action**. More often than not, the default action is `create`, but again, you will want to consult the documentation for the resource you are working with to make sure that you know what the default behavior is for a resource. You don't want to accidentally destroy something you thought you were creating!

A concrete example might be installing the `tcpdump` package on your system. To install the default version with no customization, you could use a resource description such as the following:

```
package "tcpdump"
```

This works because the default action of the package resource is to perform an installation. If you look at the source code for the package resource, you will see the following at the beginning of the constructor:

```
def initialize(name, run_context=nil)
  super
  @action = :install
  @allowed_actions.push(:install, :upgrade,
                        :remove, :purge, :reconfig)
  @candidate_version = nil
  @options = nil
  @package_name = name
```

This tells us that the default action, if unspecified, is to install the package and to use the name attribute as the package name. So, the previous simple one-line resource is the same as writing out the following block:

```
package "tcpdump" do
  action :install
  package_name "tcpdump"
end
```

Here, however, `package_name` will default to the name attribute, so we do not need to provide it if the resource name is the same as the package you wish to install. Additionally, if you wanted to be more verbose with your resource description and install a specific version of the `tcpdump` package, you could rewrite the package resource to look something like the following:

```
package "tcpdump" do
  action :install
  version "X.Y.Z"
end
```

If you read the documentation for the package resource or examine the full constructor for the package class, you will see that it has a number of other attributes as well as what they do and where their default values come from. All the resources follow this form; they are simply Ruby classes that have an expected structure, which they inherit from the base resource class.

Templates

Chef dynamically configures software and hosts, and a large part of configuring UNIX-based systems and software involves configuration files. Chef provides a straightforward mechanism to generate configuration files that make it easy to combine configuration data with template files to produce the final configuration files on hosts. These templates are stored in the `templates` directory inside of a cookbook and use the ERB template language, which is a popular and easy-to-use Ruby-based template language.

Why use templates?

Without templates, your mechanism to generate configuration files would probably look something like this:

```
File.open(local_filename, 'w') do |f|
  f.write("<VirtualHost *:#{node['app']['port']}")
  ...
  f.write("</VirtualHost>")
end
```

This should be avoided for a number of reasons. First, writing configuration data this way would most likely make your recipe very cluttered and lengthy. Secondly, and more importantly, it violates Chef's declarative nature. By design, Chef provides you with the tools to describe what the recipe is doing and not how it is doing it, which makes reading and writing recipes much easier. Simpler recipes make for simpler configuration, and simpler configuration scales better because it is easier to comprehend. Handrolling a configuration file is the opposite approach; it very specifically dictates how to generate the file data. Consider the following code:

```
config_file = "#{node['postgresql']['dir']}/postgresql.conf"
pgconfig = node[:postgresql]
File.open(config_file 'w') do |f|
  f.write("port = #{pgconfig[:port]}")
  f.write("data_dir = #{pgconfig[:data_dir]}")
```

```
     f.write("listen_address = #{pgconfig[:listen_address]}")
   end
File.chown(100,100,config_file)
File.chmod(0600, config_file)
```

This code generates a PostgreSQL configuration file from the attribute hash, one line at a time. This is not only time-consuming and hard to read but potentially very error-prone. You can imagine, even if you have not previously configured any PostgreSQL servers, just how many `f.write(...)` statements could be involved in generating a full `postgresql.conf` file by hand. Contrast that with the following block that leverages the built-in `template` resource:

```
template "#{node['postgresql']['dir']}/postgresql.conf" do
  source "postgresql.conf.erb"
  owner "postgres"
  group "postgres"
  mode 0600
end
```

The preceding block could be combined with a template file that contains the following content:

```
<% node['postgresql'] sort.each do |key, value| %>
<% next if value.nil? -%>
<%= key %> = <%=
  case value
  when String
    "'#{value}'"
  when TrueClass
    'on'
  when FalseClass
    'off'
  else
    value
  end
%>
<% end %>
```

If we take our template and then apply the following attribute data as we had shown previously, then we would have generated the exact same configuration file:

```
'node' : {
  'postgresql': {
    'port': '5432',
    'listen_address': '*',
```

```
      'data_dir': '/var/lib/postgresql',
      'install_method': 'source',
      'version': '9.3'
    },
    'users' : {
      'root' : { 'group' => 'wheel' },
    }

  }
```

Only now we can use a template that is highly flexible. Our template uses the key-value combinations stored in the configuration hash to dynamically generate the `postgresql.conf` file without being changed every time a new configuration option is added to PostgreSQL.

Chef uses ERB, a template language, that is provided by the core Ruby library. ERB is widely available and requires no extra dependencies; it supports Ruby inside of templates as well as some ERB-specific template markup.

A quick ERB primer

As ERB is very well documented and widely used, this portion of the chapter serves only as a quick reference to some of the most commonly used ERB mechanisms. For more information, see the official Ruby documentation at `http://ruby-doc.org/stdlib-2.1.1/libdoc/erb/rdoc/ERB.html`.

Executing Ruby

To execute some arbitrary Ruby code, you can use the `<% %>` container. The `<%` part indicates the beginning of the Ruby code, and `%>` indicates the end of the block. The block can span multiple lines or just one single line. Examples of this are as follows:

ERB code	Output

`<%`
`[1,2,3].each do |index|`
`    puts index`
`end`
`%>`
	1
	2
	3

`<% users.collect{ |u|` `    puts u.full_name } %>`	Bob Smith Sally Flamingo

You can mix Ruby and non-Ruby code (useful to repeat blocks of non-Ruby text) as follows:

```
<% [1,2,3].each do |value| %>
Non-ruby text...
<% end %>
```

This would yield the following:

```
Non-ruby text...
Non-ruby text...
Non-ruby text...
```

Variable replacement

ERB has a syntax to replace a section of the template with the results of some Ruby code rather than relying on print statements inside your Ruby. That container is similar to the last one, with the addition of the **equal sign** inside the opening tag. It looks like `<%= %>`. Any valid Ruby code is acceptable inside this block, and the result of this code is put into the template in place of the block. Examples of this are as follows:

```
<%= @somevariable %>
<%= hash[:key] + otherhash[:other_key] %>
<%= array.join(", ") %>
```

This can be combined with the previous example to produce complex output:

```
<% [1,2,3].each do |value| %>
The value currently is <%= value %>
<% end %>
```

This would yield the following:

```
The value currently is 1
The value currently is 2
The value currently is 3
```

Using just these basic features of ERB, combined with Chef's configuration data, you can model just about any configuration file you can imagine.

The template resource

Chef provides a template resource to generate files via templates. There are three key attributes of the template resource, which are as follows:

- `path`: This specifies where to put the generated file
- `source`: This tells the resource which template file to use
- `variables`: This specifies what data to populate the template with

The `path` attribute uses the name attribute as its default value and populates the template specified by a `source` file with the data passed to it through the `variables` attribute. Templates are contained inside of the `templates` directory, which is placed inside of a cookbook; if a source is not specified, it will be expected that a file exists inside the directory with the same name as the path, which is only rooted in the `templates` directory with a `.erb` extension. Here is a simple `template` resource example:

```
template "/etc/motd" do
  variables :users => ["Bart", "Homer", "Marge"]
end
```

This resource will expect that a file exists in the template's search path (more on how that is determined in a bit) as `etc/motd.erb`, and it then exposes an array of three strings as a `users` variable and writes the results out as `/etc/motd` on the host. The corresponding MOTD template could look like the following:

```
Welcome to crabapple.mydomain.com! Our newest users are:

<% @users.each do |user| %>
  * <%= user %>
<% end %>
```

The template variables

There are two primary sources of data for a template: data passed explicitly through the resource block attributes and node configuration data. Explicit variables are user defined in the recipe and may be used to override some settings or pass in configuration that is dynamically generated inside the recipe. The node configuration data is computed by Chef at runtime and represents a snapshot of the current configuration that will be applied to the node.

Passing variables to a template

Sometimes you will need to pass data to a template from inside your recipe instead of relying on the global node attributes. Perhaps you have some logic that computes some variable data, but it doesn't belong in the node hash; Chef supports doing just this in the `template` resource. The data passed explicitly is available to the ERB template as an instance variable, prefixed in Ruby with the @ symbol. For example, consider the following recipe snippet:

```
config_hash = {
  :food => "asparagus",
```

```
    :color => "blue"
}


template "/etc/myapp.conf" do
  source "myapp.conf.erb"
  owner "root"
  mode "0664"
  variables(
    :install_path => "/opt/#{hostname}/myapp",
    :config => config_hash
  )
end
```

The `:install_path` and `:config` keys are accessible in the template as instance variables with the same name. They will be prefixed by the `@` character and could be used in a template similar to the following:

```
database_path = "<%= @install_path %>/db"
storage_path  = "<%= @install_path %>/storage"
<% config.each do |key,value| %>
<%= key %> = "<%= value %>"
<% end %>
```

Here, the template expects a specific key, `install_path`, to determine where to store the database; the key-value hash specified by `config` is then used to generate some arbitrary configuration settings in the template.

Accessing computed configurations

In addition to data passed via the `variables` attribute, a template can access a node's computed configuration data through the `node` local variable. This is accessed as a Ruby hash, which will be structured similarly to a dictionary or a hash in any other language. In our previous PostgreSQL attribute's data example, the following values were defined:

```
default['postgresql']['port'] = "5432"
default['postgresql']['listen_address'] = "*"
```

Even if no other configuration data supersedes these configuration values, there will be a `postgresql` key in the node's configuration data that contains the key's `port` and `listen_address`. Using this information, we can write a recipe that uses a template resource and a matching template like the following:

```
template "/etc/postgresql/postgresql.conf" do
  source "postgresql.conf.erb"
  owner "psql"
  mode "0600"
end
```

```
listen_addresses = '<%= node[:postgresql][:listen_address]'
port = <%= node[:postgresql][:port] %>
```

When the default attributes data is combined with the example template, the resulting `/etc/postgresql/postgresql.conf` file will have the following content:

```
listen_addresses = '*'
post = 5432
```

As previously discussed, the computed attributes hash for a given node comes from a variety of sources. Those sources include attributes files in the cookbook, role, environment, and node-level configuration values stored in Chef, each with its own level of precedence.

Searching for templates

As you have likely noticed, Chef attempts to allow you as much, or as little, specificity as you want when defining your configuration, and templates are no different. Just as the final node configuration is computed from a variety of locations, the `templates` directory has a specific search order. This allows the author of the cookbook to provide a set of default templates as well as support platform and host-specific overrides.

The `default` template directory should be used to provide default versions of the templates. Any platform- or host-specific directories are placed alongside it and will be used when appropriate. The search order for a template is as follows:

- Hostname
- Distribution version
- Distribution
- Default location

As an example, let's consider a scenario in which we applied a recipe with the `postgresql.conf.erb` template resource to a node, `db1.production.mycorp.com`, which is running Debian 6.0. Chef will then look for the following files inside of the templates directory:

- `host-db1.production.mycorp.com/postgresql.conf.erb`
- `debian-6.0/postgresql.conf.erb`
- `debian/postgresql.conf.erb`
- `default/postgresql.conf.erb`

The search is performed in that order with the first match being the chosen template, applying the highest level of specificity before the lowest (as is the pattern with other Chef mechanisms, including configuration data).

This differentiation of configuration files by host, platform, and even version is very useful. It allows you to provide a sane set of defaults while supporting host- or system-specific quirks simultaneously.

Definitions

Sometimes, you find that you are creating something repeatedly and, similar to a configuration template, you need a template to generate objects of a given type. Some examples of this might be Apache virtual hosts, a specific type of application, or anything else that is repeated a lot. This is where definitions come in, and they are stored in the `definitions` directory inside of a cookbook.

Definitions are loaded and available as named resources just as other resources such as packages, files, and so on are; the only difference is that there is no provider. You can think of them as resources and providers all in one. Subsequently, they are much more rigid and limited in scope than a normal resource would be. Here is an example definition to install Python libraries using `pip` and a `requirements.txt` file:

```
define :pip_requirements , :action => :run do
  name = params[:name]
  requirements_file = params[:requirements_file]
  pip = params[:pip]
  user = params[:user]
  group = params[:group]

  if params[:action] == :run
    script "pip_install_#{name}" do
      interpreter "bash"
      user "#{user}"
```

```
        group "#{group}"
        code <<-EOH
        #{pip} install -r #{requirements_file}
        EOH
        only_if { File.exists?("#{requirements_file}") and File.
exists?("#{pip}") }
      end
   end
end
```

Here, we are declaring a new type of definition, a pip_requirements object. This looks and behaves similarly to a resource, except that it is much simpler (and less flexible) than a resource. It has some attributes, which are loaded via the special params argument, and contains a little bit of logic wrapped around a script resource. Let's take a look at how it would be used and then see how it works:

```
pip_requirements "my_requirements" do
  pip "#{virtualenv}/bin/pip"
  user node[:app][:user]
  group node[:app][:group]
  requirements_file "#{node[:app][:src_dir]}/requirements.txt"
end
```

Here you see what looks like a resource, but is in fact a definition. As mentioned earlier, these look very similar because they behave alike. However, you must have likely noticed that the definition of pip_requirements itself did not have any sort of abstraction; there is no pluggable provider, no validation, it doesn't subclass the Resource class, among other differences. Definitions provide you with a mechanism to declare reusable chunks of code that your recipes would otherwise duplicate so that your recipe can again describe the *what*, not the *how*.

The previous example tells us that we have a pip_requirements object and that we want to pass some parameters to it, namely, the path to pip, the user and group to run pip as, and the requirements.txt file to load. These are brought into the definition through the params argument and can be accessed as any other variable data. In this case, the definition says to run bash as the specified user and group and that the script should run the equivalent of the following:

```
pip install -r /path/to/requirements.txt
```

This will happen only if pip and the /path/to/requirements.txt file exist (as indicated by the only_if guard). By creating such a definition, it can be reused any time you need to install Python modules from a specific requirements.txt file on your host.

Recipes

Recipes are where all the magic happens with Chef; they are the secret sauce, the man behind the mask. They are the workhorses of configuring hosts with Chef. Recipes are scripts written in Ruby using Chef's DSL that contain the instructions to be executed on end hosts when the Chef client is run. Every time the client is executed on the end host, a few things happen:

1. The end host makes a request to the Chef server saying, "I need to do some work".

2. The Chef server looks at the requesting host's identity and determines:
    ◦ Which recipes need to be run and in what order (the run list)
    ◦ The computed configuration data for that host

3. This information is passed back to the end host along with the necessary artifacts it needs (recipes, templates, and so on).

4. The client then combines the configuration data with the recipes and begins to execute its run list.

Developing recipes

As a developer, you will be placing your recipes inside the `recipes` directory of your cookbook. Each recipe is designed to perform a specific action or set of actions to achieve a goal such as provisioning accounts, installing and configuring a database server, custom software deployments, or just about any other action that you could perform on a server.

A key concept when developing recipes is that they should be idempotent. For those unfamiliar with the term, an idempotent operation is an operation that can be applied multiple times and have the same outcome. Consider the following recipe:

```
user "smith" do
  action :create
  system true
  comment "Agent Smith"
  uid   1000
  gid   "agents"
  home "/home/matrix"
  shell "/bin/zsh"
end
```

One would expect, from looking at this recipe, that Chef should be able to execute it once, five times, or one thousand times, and it would have the same effect as the initial application of the recipe. There would not be five or one thousand users on the host with the login name `smith`; there would be only one single user with the login name `smith`. Also, in all the runs, it would be constructed with the same UID 1000, the same group name, and so on.

Similarly, given a particular state of the system and assuming nothing has changed in between runs, subsequent client executions should produce the same, consistent ending state. In short, the Chef client should be able to run two times in a row, and if the configuration has not been updated, the system should look exactly the same after the second run as after the first run.

Recipes use provided configuration data along with the current state of the host to determine the flow and actions taken by the script. The execution of a recipe will take the system from its initial state, Sintial, to its new state, Sfinal. Well-written recipes should be idempotent such that if they're executed immediately afterwards any number of times with no configuration or stat changes, then the system should go from Sfinal to the same Sfinal with no new changes to the system. This allows you to keep your systems in a consistent state at all times, assuming that nothing goes wrong during the execution of those operations; if something does go wrong, you should be able to revert to a previously known good state.

Writing recipes

As you have already seen, cookbooks provide a way to combine relevant pieces of configuration data such as attributes, templates, resources, providers, and definitions in one place. The only reason these components exist is to support our recipes. Recipes combine resources in a certain order to produce the desired outcome; much in the same way a chef would combine ingredients according to his or her recipe to produce some delicious food. By putting all of these resources together, we can build our own recipes that range from very simple single-step recipes to multistep, multiplatform recipes.

Starting out small

A very basic recipe, as we have discussed before, might only leverage one or two resources. One of the simplest conceivable recipes is the one we used earlier to verify that our Chef-solo installation was working properly:

```
file "#{ENV['HOME']}/example.txt" do
  action :create
  content "Greetings #{ENV['USER']}!"
end
```

Here again, we are combining a single resource, the `file` resource, specifying that we want to create the file named `$HOME/example.txt`, and store the string `"Greetings $USER"` in that file. `$USER` and `$HOME` will be replaced by the environment variables, most likely the login name of the user that is executing `chef-client` and their home directory respectively (unless the environment variables have been tampered with).

Following our goal of idempotence, executing this recipe multiple times in a row will have the same effect as only running it once.

Installing a simple service

Now that we've covered a simple recipe, let's take a look at one that configures the Redis engine and uses *supervisord* to run the daemon. This recipe doesn't install Redis; instead, it defines how to configure the system to start and manage the service. It does not have any advanced logic, but merely constructs some required directories, builds a configuration file from a template, and then uses the `supervisor_service` resource to configure the daemon to run and be monitored, as shown in the following code:

```
redis_user       = node[:redis][:user]
redis_group      = node[:redis][:group]
environment_hash = {"home" => "#{node[:redis][:home]}"}

# Create the log dir and data dir
[node[:redis][:datadir], node[:redis][:log_dir]].each do |dir|
  directory dir do
    owner       redis_user
    group       redis_group
    mode        "0750"
    recursive   true
  end
end

# Generate the template from redis.conf.erb
template "#{node[:redis][:config_path]}" do
  source "redis.conf.erb"
  owner redis_user
  group redis_group
  variables({:data_dir => "#{node[:redis][:data_dir]}"})
  mode 0644
end

# Convenience variables for readability
stdout_log = "#{node[:redis][:log_dir]}/redis-stdout.log"
```

```
stderr_log = "#{node[:redis][:log_dir]}/redis-stderr.log"
redis_bin  = "#{node[:redis][:install_path]}/bin/redis-server"
redis_conf = "#{node[:redis][:config_path]}"

# Tell supervisor to enable this service, autostart it, run it as
# the redis user, and to invoke:
#    /path/to/redis-server /path/to/redis.conf
supervisor_service "redis_service" do
    action              :enable
    autostart           true
    user                "#{redis_user}"
    command             "#{redis_bin} #{redis_conf}"
    stdout_logfile      "#{stdout_log}"
    stderr_logfile      "#{stderr_log}"
    directory           "#{node[:redis][:install_path]}"
    environment         environment_hash
end
```

You will notice that in order to keep the configuration consistent, we reuse a lot of attributes. For example, the beginning of the recipe uses node[:redis][:datadir] and node[:redis][:log_dir] to ensure that the directories exist by making use of a directory resource inside of a loop; then, these are used later on to define the supervisor configuration variables (where to write logs) and the template for the config file (where to store the data). In all, this recipe is composed of four resources: two directories in the loop, one template, and one supervisor service. By the end of this run, it will have ensured the critical directories exist, Redis is configured, and a supervisor configuration file is generated (as well as poked supervisord to reload the new configuration and start the service). Again, running this multiple times, assuming no configuration changes in between runs will put the system in the exact same state. Redis will be configured according to the host properties, and supervisor will run the service.

Getting more advanced

Let's move up and take a look at a slightly more complicated, yet fairly simple, recipe from the git cookbook that installs the git client on the host. The cookbook is multiplatform, so let's talk about what it will be doing before it shows you the source. This recipe will be performing the following actions:

1. Determine which platform the end host is running on (by inspecting the node[:platform] attribute).

2. If the host is running a Debian-based distribution, it will use the package resource to install git-core.

3. If the host is a RHEL distribution, it will perform the following:

   1. Include the EPEL repository by pulling in the `epel` recipe from the `yum` cookbook if the platform version is 5.

   2. Use the package resource to install `git` (as that is the RHEL package name).

4. If the host is Windows, it will install `git` via the `windows_package` resource and instruct it to download the file located at `node[:git][:url]` (which in turn pulls from the default attributes or overridden configuration), validate that the checksum matches the one specified by `node[:git][:checksum]`, and then install it; however, this is only if the EXE is not already installed.

5. If the host is running OS X, it will leverage the `dmg_package` resource to install a `.pkg` file from a `.dmg` image. Here, the download URL, volume name, package file, checksum, and app name are all attributes that need to be provided.

6. Finally, if none of the conditions are met, it falls back to the package resource to install the `git` package in the hope that it will work.

Here is the code for this recipe:

```
case node[:platform]
when "debian", "ubuntu"
  package "git-core"
when "centos","redhat","scientific","fedora"
  case node[:platform_version].to_i
  when 5
    include_recipe "yum::epel"
  end
  package "git"
when "windows"
  windows_package "git" do
    source node[:git][:url]
    checksum node[:git][:checksum]
    action :install
    not_if { File.exists? 'C:\Program Files (x86)\Git\bin\git.exe' }
  end
when "mac_os_x"
  dmg_package "GitOSX-Installer" do
    app node[:git][:osx_dmg][:app_name]
    package_id node[:git][:osx_dmg][:package_id]
    volumes_dir node[:git][:osx_dmg][:volumes_dir]
    source node[:git][:osx_dmg][:url]
    checksum node[:git][:osx_dmg][:checksum]
```

```
      type "pkg"
      action :install
   end
else
   package "git"
end
```

One thing we haven't seen yet is the use of the `not_if` qualifier. This is exactly what it looks like; if the block supplied to `not_if` returns a `true` value, the resource will not be processed. This is very useful to ensure that you don't clobber important files or repeat expensive operations such as recompiling a software package.

Summary

This chapter introduced you to the critical components of a cookbook that are used to write recipes. It also showed you some example recipes to get you started; there are a number of advanced actions that can be accomplished in your recipes, such as searching the Chef server for data, loading data from data bags, or using encrypted data. Additionally, you can add more components to your cookbooks such as custom resources and providers, tests, and arbitrary Ruby libraries. All of these will be discussed in detail in later chapters, but first let's take a look at writing some complete cookbooks. We'll then learn how to test them before we move on to looking at some cookbooks for common system administration tasks, and then we'll progress on to advanced topics.

Testing Your Recipes

5

So far, you have seen how to model your infrastructure, provision hosts in the cloud, and what goes into a cookbook. One important aspect of developing cookbooks is writing tests so that your recipes do not degrade over time or have bugs introduced into them in the future. This chapter introduces you to the following concepts:

- Understanding test methodologies
- How RSpec structures your tests
- Using ChefSpec to test recipes
- Running your tests
- Writing tests that cover multiple platforms

These techniques will prove to be very useful to write robust, maintainable cookbooks that you can use to confidently manage your infrastructure. Tests enable you to perform the following:

- Identify mistakes in your recipe logic
- Test your recipes against multiple platforms locally
- Develop recipes faster with local test execution before running them on a host
- Catch the changes in dependencies that will otherwise break your infrastructure before they get deployed
- Write tests for bugs to prevent them from happening again in the future (regression)

Testing recipes

There are a number of ways to test your recipes. One approach is to simply follow the process of developing your recipes, uploading them to your Chef server, and deploying them to a host; repeat this until you are satisfied. This has the benefit of executing your recipes on real instances, but the drawback is that it is slow, particularly if you are testing on multiple platforms, and requires that you maintain a fleet of hosts. If your cookbook run times are reasonably short and you have a small number of platforms to support them, then this might be a viable option. There is a better option to test your recipes, and it is called ChefSpec. For those who have used RSpec, a Ruby testing library, these examples will be a natural extension of RSpec. If you have never used RSpec, the beginning of this chapter will introduce you to RSpec's testing language and mechanisms.

RSpec

RSpec is a framework to test Ruby code that allows you to use a domain-specific language to provide tests, much in the same way Chef provides a domain-specific language to manipulate an infrastructure. Instead of using a DSL to manage systems, RSpec's DSL provides a number of components to express the expectations of code and simulate the execution of portions of the system (also known as mocking).

The following examples in RSpec should give you a high-level idea of what RSpec can do:

```
# simple expectation
it 'should add 2 and 2 together' do
  x = 2 + 2
  expect(x).to eq 4
end


# Ensure any instance of Object receives a call to 'foo'
# and return a pre-defined value (mocking)
it 'verifies that an instance receives :foo' do
  expect_any_instance_of(Object)
    .to receive(:foo).and_return(:return_value)

  o = Object.new
  expect(o.foo).to eq(:return_value)
end


# Deep expectations (i.e client makes an HTTP call somewhere
# inside it, make sure it happens as expected)
it 'should make an authorized HTTP GET call' do
```

```
expect_any_instance_of(Net::HTTP::Get)
  .to receive(:basic_auth)
@client.make_http_call
end
```

RSpec and ChefSpec

As with most testing libraries, RSpec enables you to construct a set of expectations, build objects and interact with them, and verify that the expectations have been met. For example, one expects that when a user logs in to the system, a database record is created, tracking their login history. However, to keep tests running quickly, the application should not make an actual database call; in place of the actual database call, a mock method should be used. Here, our mock method will catch the message in the database in order to verify that it was going to be sent; then, it will return an expected result so that the code does not know the database is not really there.

> Mock methods are methods that are used to replace one call with another; you can think of them as stunt doubles. For example, rather than making your code actually connect to the database, you might want to write a method that acts as though it has successfully connected to the database and fetched the expected data.

This can be extended to model Chef's ability to handle multiple platforms and environments very nicely; code should be verified to behave as expected on multiple platforms without having to execute recipes on those platforms. This means that you can test the expectations about Red Hat recipes from an OS X development machine or Windows recipes from an Ubuntu desktop, without needing to have hosts around to deploy to for testing purposes. Additionally, the development cycle time is greatly reduced as tests can be executed much faster with expectations than when they are performing some work on an end host.

You may be asking yourself, "How does this replace testing on an actual host?" The answer is that it may not, and so you should use integration testing to validate that the recipes work when deployed to real hosts. What it does allow you to do is validate your expectations of what resources are being executed, which attributes are being used, and that the logical flow of your recipes are behaving properly before you push your code to your hosts. This forms a tighter development cycle for rapid development of features while providing a longer, more formal loop to ensure that the code behaves correctly in the wild.

If you are new to testing software, and in particular, testing Ruby code, this is a brief introduction to some of the concepts that we will cover. Testing can happen at many different levels of the software life cycle:

- Single-module level (called unit tests)
- Multi-module level (known as functional tests)
- System-level testing (also referred to as integration testing)

Testing basics

In the **test-driven-development** (TDD) philosophy, tests are written and executed early and often, typically, even before code is written. This guarantees that your code conforms to your expectations from the beginning and does not regress to a previous state of non-conformity. This chapter will not dive into the TDD philosophy and continuous testing, but it will provide you with enough knowledge to begin testing the recipes that you write and feel confident that they will do the correct thing when deployed into your production environment.

Comparing RSpec with other testing libraries

RSpec is designed to provide a more expressive testing language. This means that the syntax of an RSpec test (also referred to as a spec test or spec) is designed to create a language that feels more like a natural language, such as English. For example, using RSpec, one could write the following:

```
expect(factorial(4)).to eq 24
```

If you read the preceding code, it will come out like *expect factorial of 4 to equal 24*. Compare this to a similar JUnit test (for Java):

```
assertEquals(24, factorial(4));
```

If you read the preceding code, it would sound more like *assert that the following are equal, 24 and factorial of 4*. While this is readable by most programmers, it does not feel as natural as the one we saw earlier.

RSpec also provides `context` and `describe` blocks that allow you to group related examples and shared expectations between examples in the group to help improve organization and readability. For example, consider the following spec test:

```
describe Array do
  it "should be empty when created" do
    Array.new.should == []
  end
end
```

Compare the preceding test to a similar NUnit (.NET testing framework) test:

```
namespace MyTest {
  using System.Collection
  using NUnit.Framework;
  [TestFixture]
  public class ArrayTest {
    [Test]
    public void NewArray() {
      ArrayList list = new ArrayList();
      Assert.AreEqual(0, list.size());
    }
  }
}
```

Clearly, the spec test is much more concise and easier to read, which is a goal of RSpec.

Using ChefSpec

ChefSpec brings the expressiveness of RSpec to Chef cookbooks and recipes by providing Chef-specific primitives and mechanisms on top of RSpec's simple testing language. For example, ChefSpec allows you to say things like:

```
it 'creates a file' do
  expect(chef_run).to create_file('/tmp/myfile.txt')
end
```

Here, `chef_run` is an instance of a fully planned Chef client execution on a designated end host, as we will see later. Also, in this case, it is expected that it will create a file, `/tmp/myfile.txt`, and the test will fail if the simulated run does not create such a file.

Getting started with ChefSpec

In order to get started with ChefSpec, create a new cookbook directory (here it is `$HOME/cookbooks/mycookbook`) along with a `recipes` and `spec` directory:

mkdir -p ~/cookbooks/mycookbook

mkdir -p ~/cookbooks/mycookbook/recipes

mkdir -p ~/cookbooks/mycookbook/spec

Now you will need a simple `metadata.rb` file inside your cookbook (here, this will be `~/cookbooks/mycookbook/metadata.rb`):

```
maintainer        "Your name here"
maintainer_email  "you@domain.com"
license           "Apache"
description       "Simple cookbook"
long_description  "Super simple cookbook"
version           "1.0"
supports          "debian"
```

Once we have this, we now have the bare bones of a cookbook that we can begin to add recipes and tests to.

Installing ChefSpec

In order to get started with ChefSpec, you will need to install a gem that contains the ChefSpec libraries and all the supporting components. Not surprisingly, that gem is named `chefspec` and can be installed simply by running the following:

```
gem install chefspec
```

However, because Ruby gems often have a number of dependencies, the Ruby community has built a tool called **Bundler** to manage gem versions that need to be installed. Similar to how RVM provides interpreter-level version management and a way to keep your gems organized, Bundler provides gem-level version management. We will use Bundler for two reasons. In this case, we want to limit the number of differences between the versions of software you will be installing and the versions the author has installed to ensure that things are as similar as possible; secondly, this extends well to releasing production software—limiting the number of variables is critical to consistent and reliable behavior.

Locking your dependencies in Ruby

Bundler uses a file, specifically named `Gemfile`, to describe the gems that your project is dependent upon. This file is placed in the root of your project, and its contents inform Bundler which gems you are using, what versions to use, and where to find gems so that it can install them as needed.

For example, here is the Gemfile that is being used to describe the gem versions that are used when writing these examples:

```
source 'https://rubygems.org'

gem 'chef',      '11.10.0'
gem 'chefspec',  '3.2.0'
gem 'colorize',  '0.6.0'
```

Using this will ensure that the gems you install locally match the ones that are used when writing these examples. This should limit the differences between your local testing environments if you run these examples on your workstation.

In order to use a Gemfile, you will need to have Bundler installed. If you are using RVM, Bundler should be installed with every gemset you create; if not, you will need to install it on your own via the following code:

```
gem install bundler
```

Once Bundler is installed and a `Gemfile` that contains the previous lines is placed in the root directory of your cookbook, you can execute `bundle install` from inside your cookbook's directory:

```
user@host:~/cookbooks/mycookbook $> bundle install
```

Bundler will parse the Gemfile in order to download and install the versions of the gems that are defined inside. Here, Bundler will install `chefspec`, `chef`, and `colorize` along with any dependencies those gems require that you do not already have installed.

Creating a simple recipe and a matching ChefSpec test

Once these dependencies are installed, you will want to create a spec test inside your cookbook and a matching recipe. In keeping with the TDD philosophy, we will first create a file, `default_spec.rb`, in the `spec` directory. The name of the spec file should match the name of the recipe file, only with the addition of `_spec` at the end. If you have a recipe file named `default.rb` (which most cookbooks will), the matching spec test would be contained in a file named `default_spec.rb`. Let's take a look at a very simple recipe and a matching ChefSpec test.

Writing a ChefSpec test

The test, shown as follows, will verify that our recipe will create a new file, `/tmp/myfile.txt`:

```
require 'chefspec'

describe 'mycookbook::default' do
  let(:chef_run) {
    ChefSpec::Runner.new.converge(described_recipe)
  }

  it 'creates a file' do
    expect(chef_run).to create_file('/tmp/myfile.txt')
  end
end
```

Here, RSpec uses a `describe` block similar to the way Chef uses a `resource` block (again, blocks are identified by the `do ... end` syntax or code contained inside curly braces) to describe a resource, in this case, the `default` recipe inside of `mycookbook`. The described resource has a number of examples, and each example is described by an `it` block such as the following, which comes from the previous spec test:

```
it 'creates a file' do
  expect(chef_run).to create_file('/tmp/myfile.txt')
end
```

The string given to the `it` block provides the example with a human-readable description of what the example is testing; in this case, we are expecting that the recipe creates a file. When our recipes are run through ChefSpec, the resources described are not actually created or modified. Instead, a model of what would happen is built as the recipes are executed. This means that ChefSpec can validate that an expected action would have occurred if the recipe were to be executed on an end host during a real client run.

> It's important to note that each example block resets expectations before it is executed, so any expectations defined inside of a given test will not fall through to other tests.

Because most of the tests will involve simulating a Chef client run, we want to run the simulation every time. There are two options: execute the code in every example or use a shared resource that all the tests can take advantage of. In the first case, the test will look something like the following:

```
it 'creates a file' do
  chef_run = ChefSpec::Runner.new.converge(described_recipe)
  expect(chef_run).to create_file('/tmp/myfile.txt')
end
```

The primary problem with this approach is remembering that every test will have to have the resource running at the beginning of the test. This translates to a large amount of duplicated code, and if the client needs to be configured differently, then the code needs to be changed for all the tests. To solve this problem, RSpec provides access to a shared resource through a built-in method, `let`. Using `let` allows a test to define a shared resource that is cached for each example and reset as needed for the following examples. This resource is then accessible inside of each block as a local variable, and RSpec takes care of knowing when to initialize it as needed.

Our example test uses a `let` block to define the `chef_run` resource, which is described as a new ChefSpec runner for the described recipe, as shown in the following code:

```
let(:chef_run) {
  ChefSpec::Runner.new.converge(described_recipe)
}
```

Here, `described_recipe` is a ChefSpec shortcut for the name of the recipe provided in the describe block. Again, this is a DRY (don't repeat yourself) mechanism that allows us to rename the recipe and then only have to change the name of the description rather than hunt through the code. These techniques make tests better able to adapt to changes in names and resources, which reduces code rot as time goes by.

Building your recipe

The recipe, as defined here, is a very simple recipe whose only job is to create a simple file, `/tmp/myfile.txt`, on the end host:

```
file "/tmp/myfile.txt" do
  owner "root"
  group "root"
  mode "0755"
  action :create
end
```

Put this recipe into the `recipes/default.rb` file of your cookbook so that you have the following file layout:

```
mycookbook/
  |- recipes/
  |     |- default.rb
  |- spec/
        |- default_spec.rb
```

Executing tests

In order to run the tests, we use the `rspec` application. This is a Ruby script that comes with the RSpec gem, which will run the test scripts as spec tests using the RSpec language. It will also use the ChefSpec extensions because in our spec test, we have included them via the line `require 'chefspec'` at the top of our `default_spec.rb` file. Here, `rspec` is executed through Bundler to ensure that the desired gem versions, as specified in our `Gemfile`, are used at runtime without having to explicitly load them. This is done using the `bundle exec` command:

```
bundle exec rspec spec/default_spec.rb
```

This will run RSpec using Bundler and process the `default_spec.rb` file. As it runs, you will see the results of your tests, a . (period) for tests that pass, and an F for any tests that fail. Initially, the output from `rspec` will look like this:

```
Finished in 0.17367 seconds

1 example, 0 failures
```

RSpec says that it completed the execution in 0.17 seconds and that you had one example with zero failures. However, the results would be quite different if we have a failed test; RSpec will tell us which test failed and why.

Understanding failures

RSpec is very good at telling you what went wrong with your tests; it doesn't do you any good to have failing tests if it's impossible to determine what went wrong. When an expectation in your test is not met, RSpec will tell you which expectation was unmet, what the expected value was, and what value was seen.

In order to see what happens when a test fails, modify your recipe to ensure that the test fails. Look in your recipe for the following file resource:

```
file "/tmp/myfile.txt" do
```

Replace the file resource with a different filename, such as `myfile2.txt`, instead of `myfile.txt`, like the following example:

```
file "/tmp/myfile2.txt" do
```

Next, rerun your spec tests; you will see that the test is now failing because the simulated Chef client execution did something that was unexpected by our spec test. An example of this new execution would look like the following:

```
[user@host]$ bundle exec rspec spec/default_spec.rb
F


Failures:


  1) my_cookbook::default creates a file
     Failure/Error: expect(chef_run).to create_file('/tmp/myfile.txt')
       expected "file[/tmp/myfile.txt]" with action :create to be in Chef
run. Other file resources:


         file[/tmp/myfile2.txt]


     # ./spec/default_spec.rb:9:in `block (2 levels) in <top (required)>'


Finished in 0.18071 seconds
1 example, 1 failure
```

Notice that instead of a dot, the test results in an F; this is because the test is now failing. As you can see from the previous output, RSpec is telling us the following:

- The `creates a file` example in the `'my_cookbook::default'` test suite failed
- Our example failed in the ninth line of `default_spec.rb` (as indicated by the line that contained `./spec/default_spec.rb:9`)
- The file resource `/tmp/myfile.txt` was expected to be operated on with the `:create` action
- The recipe interacted with a file resource `/tmp/myfile2.txt` instead of `/tmp/myfile.txt`

RSpec will continue to execute all the tests in the files specified on the command line, printing out their status as to whether they passed or failed. If your tests are well written and run in isolation, then they will have no effect on one another; it should be safe to execute all of them even if some fail so that you can see what is no longer working.

Expanding your tests

ChefSpec provides a comprehensive suite of tools to test your recipes; you can stub and mock resources (replace real behavior with artificial behavior, such as network or database connections), simulate different platforms, and more. Let's take a look at some more complex examples to see what other things we can do with ChefSpec.

Multiple examples in a spec test

Spec tests do not need to contain only one example; they can contain as many as you need. In order to organize them, you can group them together by what they describe and some shared context. In RSpec, context blocks contain examples that are relevant to the recipe or script being tested. Think of them as self-contained test suites within a larger test suite; they can have their own resources as well as setup and tear-down logic that are specific to the tests that are run in that context.

As an example, let's look at part of the spec test suite from the `render_file` example inside of ChefSpec itself. Consider this portion of the recipe:

```
file '/tmp/file' do
  content 'This is content!'
end

cookbook_file '/tmp/cookbook_file' do
  source 'cookbook_file'
end

template '/tmp/template' do
  source 'template.erb'
end
```

The recipe being shown has three resources: a template, a `cookbook_file`, and an ordinary file resource. A sample of the matching spec test (tests removed for formatting and ease of reading) contains an outer `describe` block, which tells us that we are executing tests for the `render_file::default` recipe and three separate context blocks. Each context describes a different portion of the recipe that is being tested and the expectations of that particular type of resource. Together, they are all part of the default recipe, but they behave very differently in what content they render as well as where and how they store files on the system.

In this example, the `file` context contains tests that pertain to the expected results of the `file` resource, the `cookbook_file` context is concerned with the `cookbook_file` resource, and so on:

```
describe 'render_file::default' do
  let(:chef_run) {
    ChefSpec::Runner.new.converge(described_recipe)
  }

  context 'file' do
    it 'renders the file' do
      expect(chef_run).to render_file('/tmp/file')
      expect(chef_run).to_not render_file('/tmp/not_file')
    end
  end

  context 'cookbook_file' do
    it 'renders the file' do
      expect(chef_run).to render_file('/tmp/cookbook_file')
      expect(chef_run).to_not
              render_file('/tmp/not_cookbook_file')
    end
  end

  context 'template' do
    it 'renders the file' do
      expect(chef_run).to render_file('/tmp/template')
      expect(chef_run).to_not render_file('/tmp/not_template')
    end
  end

end
```

Contexts can be used to group together a set of examples that are related, not just ones that are specific to a particular resource. Consider the following example:

```
describe 'package::install' do
  context 'when installing on Windows 2012' do
  end
  context 'when installing on Debian' do
  end
  context 'when installing on FreeBSD' do
  end
end
```

In the previous example, our spec test contained tests that are grouped together by the platform being executed on. Inside of each context, the Chef run will be constructed with a `platform` argument instead so that the expectations being tested will be considered against a run of the recipe on the platform in question rather than the host's operating system. This is incredibly useful, as we will see in the next section on testing for multiple platforms.

Testing for multiple platforms

One of the more non-trivial uses of ChefSpec is to simulate executing recipes on multiple platforms. This is useful for developers who are building recipes that need to support more than one operating system. Software packages such as PostgreSQL, MySQL, Java, PHP, Apache, and countless other applications can be installed on many different platforms. Because each platform varies in its installation mechanism, user creation, and other core features, being able to test recipes against all the supported platforms is incredibly useful.

Let's look at a hypothetical example to develop a recipe to install MySQL on Windows 2012 and some things we might want to validate during such a run:

```
context 'when run on Windows 2012' do
  let(:chef_run) do
    # construct a 'runner' (simulate chef-client) running
    # on a Windows 2012 host
    runner = ChefSpec::ChefRunner.new(
        'platform' => 'windows',
        'version' => '2012'
    )
    # set a configuration variable
    runner.node.set['mysql']['install_path'] = 'C:\\temp'
    runner.node.set['mysql']['service_user'] = 'SysAppUser'
    runner.converge('mysql::server')
  end

  it 'should include the correct Windows server recipe' do
    chef_run.should include_recipe 'mysql::server_windows'
  end

  it 'should create an INI file in the right directory' do
    ini_file = "C:\\temp\\mysql\\mysql.ini"
    expect(chef_run).to create_template ini_file
  end
end
```

By constructing the **runner** with the `platform` and `version` options, the test will exercise running the `mysql::server` recipe and pretend as though it were running on a Windows 2012 host. This allows us to set up expectations about the templates that will be created, recipes that are being executed, and more on that particular platform.

Presuming that the `mysql::server` recipe was able to delegate to the OS-specific recipe on a given platform, we could write another test:

```
context 'when run on Debian' do
  let(:chef_run) do
    runner = ChefSpec::ChefRunner.new(
        'platform' => 'debian'
    )
    runner.node.set['mysql']['install_path'] = '/usr/local'
    runner.node.set['mysql']['service_user'] = 'mysql'
    runner.converge('mysql::server')
  end

  it 'should include the correct Linux server recipe' do
    chef_run.should include_recipe 'mysql::server_linux'
  end

  it 'should create an INI file in the right directory' do
    ini_file = "/usr/local/mysql/mysql.ini"
    expect(chef_run).to create_template ini_file
  end

  it 'should install the Debian MySQL package' do
    expect(chef_run).to install_package('mysql-server')
  end
end
```

In this way, we can write our tests to validate the expected behavior on platforms that we may not have direct access to in order to ensure that they will be performing the expected actions for a collection of platforms.

Summary

RSpec with ChefSpec extensions provides us with incredibly powerful tools to test our cookbooks and recipes. You have seen how to develop basic ChefSpec tests for your recipes, organize your spec tests inside of your cookbook, execute and analyze the output of your spec tests, and simulate the execution of your recipes across multiple platforms.

In future chapters, we will learn some more advanced testing mechanisms such as mocking and stubbing external services such as search and data bags. Adding testing to your development cycle allows you to feel confident in the correctness of your recipes, which is a critical step towards automating the management of your infrastructure.

Now, let's take a look at how we will build a cookbook to complement a web application so that we can see the full cycle of developing an application and deploying it using Chef.

6

From Development to Deployment

This chapter covers end-to-end software deployment of a Python-based web application. It will also introduce you to some common cookbooks and how to put them all together to create a fully automated deployment mechanism.

We will walk through the following topics:

- Configuring your local settings to work with AWS
- Modeling a simple web.py application with Chef
- Installing the cookbooks you need
- Provisioning EC2 instances for web and DB servers
- Defining your roles
- Adding users to hosts
- Installing the required software
- Configuring an application using Chef
- Deploying the application

Describing the setup

From a high level, here is what needs to happen in order to take an application that we have developed from a desktop to deployment. In order to deploy your application, you will provision two hosts, `web` and `db` (each with one user account) and `webapp`, whose home directory will be in `/home/webapp`. The source code will be hosted on GitHub and deployed using Git onto the web server. We will create a database, provision an account to access that database, and then configure and deploy a `web.py` application in a virtual Python environment that will be started and monitored by supervisord. This is a fairly common pattern for modern web applications, regardless of the framework and language being used. The demonstration application used in this chapter consists of only a handful of files making it easy to deploy and understand, but this will give you the concepts and tools to expand this example for use with future applications you might develop or need to deploy.

Deploying software with Chef

There are numerous benefits to deploying your software using Chef; the primary benefit is automation—the chef-client can be run periodically, and it can execute fully-automated deployments whenever changes are made to the source code repository. Additionally, Chef stores all your configuration data, so you can avoid storing sensitive secrets and hard-coding URLs or other dynamic data in your configuration. For example, if you have an application with a database pool, and you add a new database host to your pool, Chef can use a simple search to populate the list of hosts to include in the connection pool so that it is always up to date with your infrastructure.

However, deploying software with Chef does require some coordination between your application and Chef. You will need to maintain recipes required for deploying your application, and you will also want to use Chef as the authoritative source for your configuration data, which involves writing configuration templates. By using Chef to manage your deployments, you can also generate any configuration data needed to run your software based on your infrastructure configuration; in our case, a simple `config.py` file for your `web.py` application. This method can also be used to manage the `database.yml` file (and any other YAML files) for Rails applications, the `server.yml` file for a Dropwizard application, or any other configuration files needed to run your service.

 YAML is a simple markup language to store configuration data. It is popular with modern developers because it is easy to parse and is very expressive, similar to JSON.

Configuring your local environment

By now, you should have access to a Chef server of some sort; here, we will be using the hosted Chef service, but the work (aside from configuring your `knife.rb` file) will remain the same across self-managed and hosted Chef instances. In order to follow along with the examples, you will need to configure your workstation with an appropriate `knife.rb` file and certificates. These files can be downloaded from the hosted Chef console and modified as needed.

Additionally, you will need to have installed `knife` through the `chef` gem and have the `knife-ec2` gem installed in order to interact with EC2. If you prefer to use a different provider, then you can refer to the previous chapter on how to provision cloud hosts with this provider when you get to the provisioning step.

In our example, using hosted Chef and EC2, our `knife.rb` file will contain content similar to the following code:

```
current_dir = File.dirname(__FILE__)
log_level       :info
log_location    STDOUT
node_name       "myorg"
client_key      "#{current_dir}/myorg.pem"
validation_client_name "myorg-validator"
validation_key  "#{current_dir}/myorg-validator.pem"
chef_server_url "https://api.opscode.com/organizations/myorg"
cache_type      'BasicFile'
cache_options( :path => "#{ENV['HOME']}/.chef/checksums" )
cookbook_path   ["#{current_dir}/../cookbooks"]

knife[:aws_access_key_id] = "YOUR AWS ACCESS KEY"
knife[:aws_secret_access_key] = "YOUR AWS SECRET KEY"
knife[:region] = "AWS REGION"
```

Again, the base files can be downloaded from the hosted Chef console, or if you are using a self-managed Chef installation, this can be found on your Chef server.

Modeling a simple Python application

Here we will consider a `web.py` application that has two primary components: a web server and a database server. We will provision one host for each role, bootstrap them, and deploy the software onto our new hosts.

Our application stack will consist of the following:

- `web.py` as our web framework
- PostgreSQL for data storage
- EC2 for virtual hosts

We want to define two primary roles that represent our web server and our database server. In addition, we will construct a **baseline** role for all our servers that will supply any common data we need such as user accounts, SSH keys, network configuration data, shells, common utilities, libraries, and so on.

We will need to find or write cookbooks for the following components we will use:

- Python
- supervisord
- PostgreSQL
- User accounts
- Our custom web application

Managing the cookbooks

The cookbooks that we will be using are all available at the following URL: `https://github.com/johnewart/simplewebpy_app`. Because a number of cookbooks used in this example are under active development, the ones required for the examples have been frozen (as of writing of this book) to ensure compatibility with the examples; it is better to have them slightly out of date than broken in this case.

However, when you write your own cookbooks and deploy your own software beyond this example, you will find that there are a large number of cookbooks that can be found through the Chef community site—`http://supermarket.getchef.com/`—or by searching the Web for cookbooks; many of these will be hosted on GitHub, BitBucket, or similar source code-hosting sites.

Downloading cookbooks

Here in the following code, we will simply download the cookbook collection as a whole:

```
http://github.com/johnewart/chef_essential_files
```

To install the collection, we can do the following from the `chef_essential_files/cookbooks` directory:

```
knife cookbook install -o . *
```

This will install all of the cookbooks that are provided. The provided cookbooks are all that is required for the examples in this chapter to be successful. Let's take a look at our custom cookbook, the `pythonwebapp` cookbook, as all of the others are off-the-shelf cookbooks that are designed to provide some general support functionalities.

Looking at the database recipe

We will do a few things here, so let's look at our `database` recipe. In order for our web application to be useful, it needs a database to connect to. Typically, this involves installing the database server software, constructing a database, and granting access to that database by a specified user (or users). Our application is no different, so we will leverage the `database` cookbook in order to accomplish this.

First, in our recipe, we need to include the PostgreSQL-specific resources from the `database` cookbook, which we will do using the following code:

```
include_recipe "database::postgresql"
```

You will need to know what database you will be creating and to which user you will be granting access to along with the password that will be used to identify them:

```
dbname = node[:webapp][:dbname]
dbuser = node[:webapp][:dbuser]
dbpass = node[:webapp][:dbpass]
```

In order to create a database and user as well as grant access, you will need to establish a connection to the database server with a user that has permission to do so. You will see that this user has also been granted access in your role's `pg_hba` settings so that PostgreSQL knows to allow the `postgres` user to connect to the database locally, as shown in the following code:

```
postgresql_connection_info = {
  :host     => 'localhost',
  :port     => node['postgresql']['config']['port'],
  :username => 'postgres',
  :password => node['postgresql']['password']['postgres']
}
```

Using this connection information, you can construct a database and a user (if they don't already exist), and then grant that user full access to our new database:

```
# Construct an actual database on the server
postgresql_database 'webapp' do
  connection postgresql_connection_info
  action     :create
end

# Create a database user resource using our connection
postgresql_database_user dbuser do
  connection postgresql_connection_info
  password   dbpass
  action     :create
end

# Grant all privileges on all tables in 'webapp'
postgresql_database_user dbuser do
  connection    postgresql_connection_info
  database_name dbname
  privileges    [:all]
  action        :grant
end
```

This high-level language allows us to easily manipulate the database without the need to know any database-specific SQL or commands. If you want to convert your application to use MySQL, for example, provisioning a new MySQL database would largely be as easy as converting the word **postgresql** to **mysql** in our recipe, and the database-specific adapter in the `database` cookbook will be responsible for the implementation details.

Looking at your application deployment cookbook

Once our database has been provisioned, you can look at how you can install our web application. In the `pythonwebapp::webapp` recipe, you have all the information you need to do this. The way that you define a recipe for deploying an application will vary wildly among applications, as each application is unique. However, this particular example was designed to be a representative of most web applications (reasonably) and should present you with a good starting point to understand the basics of deploying a web application with Chef.

Modern web applications typically follow the same pattern: provision a user, install an interpreter, or other engine (such as Python, Ruby, and Java), create directories if needed, check out the source code, run any data migrations (if needed) to update your database, and then make sure that your service is up and running; this is no different. The more complicated your application, the more infrastructure you may need to model, such as job queue engines, asynchronous workers, and other libraries.

If you look at the web application cookbook located at `cookbooks/pythonwebapp`, you will see that it has the following: two recipes, a template, and a PIP-requirement definition inside it. The recipes included are for the web application itself and to manage the creation of the PostgreSQL database and user on the database host.

Most of the interesting work is in the application recipe, `cookbooks/pythonwebapp/recipes/webapp.rb`; so, let's start by taking a look at that. All applications are going to have a slightly different deployment logic, but modern web applications usually follow a pattern that looks like the following:

- Install any system-wide packages required
- Construct the directories needed for the software
- If this is Python or Ruby, possibly install a new `virtualenv` tool or RVM gemset
- Install the libraries needed to run the application
- Check out the application's source code
- Build and configure the application as needed
- Create or update the database schema
- Stop the web application services
- Start the web server or process manager that monitors the application

This example application is no different, so let's look at the steps needed to deploy this `web.py` application. First, declare any application configuration data needed with the following command:

```
app_root = node[:webapp][:install_path]
python_interpreter = node[:webapp][:python]
virtualenv = "#{app_root}/python"
virtual_python = "#{virtualenv}/bin/python"
src_dir = "#{app_root}/src/"
# Grab the first database host
```

```
dbhost = search(:node, "role:postgresql_server")[0]['ipaddress']

environment_hash = {
  "HOME" => "#{app_root}",
  "PYTHONPATH" => "#{app_root}/src"
}
```

In this snippet, we used the computed attributes to tell our recipe where to install the application; in this case, the default is /opt/webapp but this can be overridden for flexibility. Additionally, we set the path to the Python interpreter we want to use for our Python virtualenv. However, you can just as easily specify a Ruby or Java path if your application used one of those languages. There is a path to the source code and a database host address. This path is determined by searching the Chef data for all nodes with the postgresql_server role, taking the first one, and using its IP. This allows us to replace the database server and not have to worry about updating our configuration data, which we'll see in a bit.

Preparing the directories

In order to deploy our application, and for it to run, we need to have a location to put our data. In this application, we have defined a need for: a configuration directory, a log directory, and a place to view the source code. In our recipe, we will create these directories and set proper ownership to our deployment user and group. Note that you do not need to create the application root directory if it already exists, and you do not need to set special ownership or permissions on the root directory. Because we are leveraging the recursive property of the directory resource, the root application directory will be implicitly created; however, we are constructing it here for the sake of completeness.

It is critical that our directories have the correct ownership and permissions; without this, the application will be unable to interact with those directories to store log data or read-and-write any configuration data. The following code constructs these directories for us and changes the ownership and permissions:

```
directory "#{app_root}" do
  owner node[:webapp][:user]
  group node[:webapp][:group]
  mode "0755"
  action :create
  recursive true
end

# Create directories
["src", "logs", "conf"].each do |child_dir|
```

```
    directory "#{app_root}/#{child_dir}" do
      owner node[:webapp][:user]
      group node[:webapp][:group]
      mode "0755"
      action :create
      recursive true
    end
  end
```

One thing to note here is that we are using a loop to construct our directories. This is a good way to manage multiple resources of the same type that have the same set of configuration parameters. Here we are saying that we have three subdirectories, src, log, and conf. Also, we want to construct a directory resource inside of our application's root directory for each subdirectory with proper ownership and permissions. The recursive flag is similar to the -p option on mkdir, which tells it to create any directories that are missing in between the root and the directory being created.

Constructing your Python virtual environment

This may be new to non-Python developers but should be fairly straightforward. A virtual environment operates in a similar way to RVM or rbenv for Ruby, or a self-contained JAR file for Java. In that, it isolates the Python interpreter and installed libraries to a specific location on the system. In our case, we will use the following code to achieve this:

```
    python_virtualenv "#{virtualenv}" do
      owner node[:webapp][:user]
      group node[:webapp][:group]
      action :create
      interpreter "#{python_interpreter}"
    end
```

This python_virtualenv resource comes from the python cookbook and will construct a virtual environment in the location named by the resource (in our case, the directory stored in virtualenv, which as we saw previously, is defined as though in a python directory inside our application root) using the specified interpreter and ownership properties.

A virtual environment will be created, which contains a minimal installation of the Python interpreter as well as any Python libraries that are installed into the virtual environment. Think of it as your application's own installation of Python that is unaffected by, and subsequently does not affect, any other Python installation on the system.

This is a very useful technique to install and manage Python applications, and the same concept can be extended to the Rails application using any similar technology from the Ruby world such as RVM or `rbenv`, as mentioned earlier.

Checking the source code

One interesting thing in this recipe, which has been included for future reference, is the usage of a cookbook, `ssh_known_hosts`, that grabs a host's SSH key and adds it to the system's list of known SSH keys. This is extremely useful to deploy software via GitHub or BitBucket, where you are using SSH to pull down the source code, especially as their host keys might change:

```
# Need to install SSH key for github.com
ssh_known_hosts_entry 'github.com'
```

Note that it is also somewhat insecure as you are blindly accepting the host's fingerprint—if you are concerned about security, you can provide the known fingerprints manually using the `:key` attribute. Supplying the fingerprint is done through the following code:

```
ssh_known_hosts_entry 'github.com' do
  key  'github.com ssh-rsa AAAAB3NzaC1yc....'
end
```

If there are a large number of host fingerprints that you need to manage, or if they change frequently, you can use a data bag to store them. If you are interested, look at the README for the `ssh_known_hosts` cookbook for more examples.

Once the SSH keys are registered, you can now clone the source from a `git+ssh` URL such as GitHub's authenticated SSH endpoint.

In this example, we are using a publicly available HTTPS source code repository; if you were to replace this with your own SSH-enabled repository, you would need to change the repository attribute and also make sure to store your deployment key on the endhost:

```
# Clone our application source
git "#{src_dir}" do
  repository "https://github.com/johnewart/simplewebpy_app.git"
  action :sync
  branch 'master'
  user node[:webapp][:user]
end
```

By using the `git` resource, the repository will be cloned into the designated source directory on the endhost. Here, we will also be pulling data from the `master` branch and performing this action as our `webapp` user.

Installing any extra dependencies

There are two ways to model dependencies for your application: in your cookbook and recipe, or through an external mechanism such as Bundler, pip, or other dependency resolution, and the downloading tool depending on the language of your choice. As with everything, there are both inherent drawbacks and benefits to each of these methods.

Managing dependencies in Chef

By modeling your dependencies in Chef, you have a consistent model that you can look to in a centralized location. This means that your application needs a new Ruby gem, or a Python library that someone must update a cookbook or Chef configuration with that information in order for the deployment to be successful. This can limit your ability to continuously deploy based solely on the contents of a source code repository. In effect, this requires you to model the following in Chef:

- Dependent libraries
- Library versions
- Possibly, the dependencies of any declared dependencies (which can spiral quickly)

However, modeling it this way does ensure that Chef has an accurate picture of all the information associated with your application. This solution does offer some other benefits:

- Dependencies are precisely modeled in Chef and can be queried by other tools
- Any system-specific packages that are needed for your interpreted libraries are going to be modeled by Chef anyway, so it's all in one place (examples can include native XML or database libraries)
- Developers can't arbitrarily change dependencies and accidentally break deployments because the underlying libraries have not been installed in production

Let's look at some things to think about when using tools external to Chef for this task.

Managing dependencies elsewhere

Using an external tool such as Bundler or pip has some advantages, including flexibility and ease of use by developers who may not be involved in infrastructure configuration. It also introduces the possibility of misconfigured dependencies and underlying libraries. The primary advantage of this mechanism is that it provides a simpler dependency management model for developers—simply add a requirement to the Gemfile, `requirements.txt`, or other metadata file, and Chef will automatically install them during the next run. You also now have to look in two different places to determine what is being installed on endhosts. This also means that you are now configuring dependencies in multiple places, increasing the possibility of making a wrong configuration change in one place.

It's important to take away that there is not always only one tool for the job, and depending on how your organization or team operates, you may choose to mix and match how you model the application-level dependencies. For the sake of demonstrating them both to you, the application cookbook models the dependencies in the recipe as well as through a `requirements.txt` file using pip. Additionally, you may find that initially your team uses one way and then moves to another as your requirements stop changing so frequently, or you are able to combine them to your advantage.

Using Python's requirements file

Our `webapp` cookbook has a custom `pip_requirements` definition that provides an easy way to install any requirements stored inside a `requirements.txt` file into a specified virtual environment using the copy of pip provided by that virtual environment. In the following code, you will see how we can achieve this:

```
pip_requirements "webapp" do
  action :run
  pip "#{virtualenv}/bin/pip"
  user node[:webapp][:user]
  group node[:webapp][:group]
  requirements_file "#{src_dir}/requirements.txt"
end
```

In this example, we are telling pip to run as our application's user and group and to install the dependencies in our `requirements.txt` into the virtual environment specified by `virtualenv`. Again, a similar resource can be created (if one does not already exist) to execute Bundler for Ruby, CPAN for Perl, or PEAR to manage PHP dependencies.

Configuring your application

Now that you have prepared your system for your application, you need to configure it. In order for the application to talk to our database, you must provide the required database connection information that we have stored in Chef. Here, we will use a template that is stored in `templates/default/config.py.erb`, and inject it with our database configuration. The resource for this looks like the following code:

```
template "#{src_dir}/config.py" do
  source "config.py.erb"
  user node[:webapp][:user]
  group node[:webapp][:group]
  mode "0600"
  variables({
    :dbname => node[:webapp][:dbname],
    :dbuser => node[:webapp][:dbuser],
    :dbpass => node[:webapp][:dbpass],
    :dbhost => dbhost
  })
end
```

Here, we load our database information onto our template and store it in our application's install directory (where we checked out the source for simplicity), and set some sane file permissions. Were this a Rails application, we can use a similar template to generate `database.yml` and matching `settings.yml`, or if it were a Dropwizard application, a `service.yml` file, a PHP INI file, or any other type of configuration data that were needed. In our case, we are simply populating the following Python code so that we have a database connection object:

```
import web
db_params = {
  'dbn': 'postgres',
  'db': '<%= @dbname %>',
  'user': '<%= @dbuser %>',
  'pw': '<%= @dbpass %>',
  'host' : '<%= @dbhost %>'
}
DB = web.database(**db_params)
cache = False
```

The previous example uses the `web.py` database module to construct a new database connection using the hash, which can then be imported and used in the other portions of the application. Again, this is a good starting example for our `web.py` application that can be used as a model for whatever framework or application server you are using in your systems.

Keeping your application running

All applications need to be started and kept running in some manner. If you are using Rails with mod_passenger, then the Apache daemon will be the primary entry point for your application, and this software will need to be installed and configured. In our example, we will be using the supervisord service from http://supervisord.org, which is written in Python and serves as a very configurable, lightweight, and reliable process manager. You can configure an entry in the supervisord system configuration using a supervisor_service resource that is provided by the supervisor cookbook installed earlier:

```
supervisor_service "webapp" do
  action                   [:enable,:restart]
  autostart                true
  user                     node[:webapp][:user]
  command                  "#{virtual_python} #{src_dir}/server.py
#{node[:webapp][:port]}"
  stdout_logfile           "#{app_root}/logs/webapp-stdout.log"
  stdout_logfile_backups   5
  stdout_logfile_maxbytes  "50MB"
  stdout_capture_maxbytes  "0"
  stderr_logfile           "#{app_root}/logs/webapp-stderr.log"
  stderr_logfile_backups   5
  stderr_logfile_maxbytes  "50MB"
  stderr_capture_maxbytes  "0"
  directory                src_dir
  environment              environment_hash
end
```

The previous example will generate a configuration file for supervisord with the settings specified in our resource block. Unless you change the location, the configuration files will be located in /etc/supervisor.d/[service_name].conf. In our case, the service is named webapp, and its configuration file will be /etc/supervisor.d/webapp.conf.

Here, we are telling supervisord that we want to enable our service and then restart it (which will start it if it's not currently running), where we want to log the process's output, how we want to rotate those log files, where to start our process, what environment variables to use, and most importantly what command to execute.

Now that we've looked at our recipes, let's go ahead and set up our roles, provision some systems, and deploy our application!

Defining roles

Here we will construct our three roles, one each for our base server configuration, database server, and web server. Each role will have a set of recipes to run, with the base server providing the user accounts, SSH keys, and other common components, and then the others providing configuration data for PostgreSQL and nginx, respectively.

Creating the base server role

The key bits that are of interest in our base server role are the run list and the configuration data that specify which group to populate users for. If you look at the file `roles/base_server.json`, you will see that we have defined one group of users to pull from our data bags:

```
"override_attributes": {
  "shell_users": {
    "group": "webapp"
  }
}
```

And then, the recipe we want to use that will populate the users on the host is in the run list:

```
"run_list": [
  "users::shell_users"
],
```

In order to load the role into Chef, you can issue a `from file` command:

```
knife role from file base_server.json
Updated Role base _server!
```

You can verify that the role was created with a simple `role list` command:

```
[user]% knife role list
base_server
```

Creating the database server role

Let's take a look at some portions of our database server role, as defined in roles/postgresql_server.json. This file contains the description of our PostgreSQL server as modeled earlier in the chapter. What is of interest in this file is our override_attributes section; these are settings we want to use in place of the default values provided by our postgresql cookbook. As mentioned before, you will want to look at the documentation and the default attributes.rb file to find out what attributes you can set for a given cookbook and its recipes.

The PostgreSQL recipes use a postgresql configuration section that contains a config section for server-specific configuration and properties, and pg_hba for the authentication data. Looking at the postgresql section, we can see that we want to install Version 9.3, and we want it to listen on all addresses (0.0.0.0) on port 5432:

```
"version": "9.3",
"config": {
  "listen_addresses": "0.0.0.0",
  "port": "5432"
},
```

In addition, the pg_hba section contains an array of JSON objects that describes which users have access to the service, by what mechanism they are able to authenticate themselves (MD5, trusted, local ident service, and so on), and from where they can connect. This is coded into our configuration, but the recipes can be extended to use data bags to determine this information as well. It is too long to include all of it here, but if you look at the pg_hba data, you will see that there are three entries: one for the user webuser to connect from anywhere using an MD5 password, and two for local users to access the default template database, and for the postgres user itself to modify the webapp database.

In addition to the configuration data, there is a run list—this tells Chef what recipes this role will include. You can see from this example that we will be installing the PostgreSQL server and then provisioning our webapp-specific user and database (found in cookbooks/pythonwebapp/recipes/database.rb):

```
"run_list": [
  "postgresql::server",
  "pythonwebapp::database"
],
```

In order to use this, we want to load our JSON file into Chef to define our database server role:

```
knife role from file postgresql_server.json
Updated Role postgresql_server!
```

You can check that the role was created with a `role list` command:

```
[user]% knife role list
base_server
postgresql_server
```

Creating the web server role

Our web application role is located in the `roles/web_server.json` file and contains the required information for our web server. If you take a look at the JSON file, you will see that the run list contains four entries:

```
"run_list": [
  "python",
  "python::virtualenv",
  "supervisor",
  "pythonwebapp::webapp"
],
```

Because our application relies on Python, we want to install the required version of Python on our hosts as well as build a Python `virtualenv` tool for our application. In addition, we will be using supervisord as the process monitor that is responsible for ensuring that our web service starts and stays running. We also need to install our web application once we have met our prerequisites.

Similar to how we loaded the PostgreSQL role from our JSON file, we can repeat the process for our web server role:

```
knife role from file web_server.json
Updated Role web_server!
```

Again, you can check that the role was created with a simple `role list` command:

```
[user]% knife role list
base_server
postgresql_server
web_server
```

Adding users

We will need a recipe to manage our users; here, we will use the `users` cookbook. We will create one user, `webuser`, which will be the account that is used for deployment and user connectivity. We will define our user in a JSON file similar to what we did in the previous chapter; place the following in a `users/webuser.json` file:

```
{
  "id" : "webuser",
  "uid" : "1000",
  "gid" : 1000,
  "shell" : "/bin/bash",
  "comment" : "Webapp deployment user",
  "groups" : ["webusers"]
}
```

Then, you can load this user using the `from file` command:

```
knife data bag from file users users
```

Ensure that your hosts have our new users by editing the `base_server` role and adding our `webusers` group so that any users in that group will be provisioned on all our servers that incorporate the `base_server` role:

```
{
  "shell_users": {
    "group": "webusers",
  }
}
```

Provisioning EC2 instances

Here, we will be provisioning instances in `us-west-1`, but depending on where you have your AWS instances set up, you will need to change your `knife.rb` configuration to specify the region of your choice.

In order for them to communicate securely, we will construct a security group so that all traffic between them is permitted. This is outside the scope of this book, but it would be something to make sure you configure for production systems, as you probably do not want the public on the Internet to have direct access to your database server.

Here, we will assume that you have your AWS credentials and other critical components configured, as we covered in previous chapters.

To provision our database server, we will use the following command:

```
knife ec2 server create -d ubuntu14.04 -I ami-ee4f77ab -f m1.small -Z us-
west-1a -S jewartec2 -N db00 --ssh-user ubuntu
```

And to provision the web server, we will use the following command:

```
knife ec2 server create -d ubuntu14.04 -I ami-ee4f77ab -f m1.small -Z us-
west-1a -S jewartec2 -N web00 --ssh-user ubuntu
```

Once your instances are up and running, you can now move on to configuring them with the roles and configuration data required!

Configuring the database host

In order to apply the PostgreSQL role to our database host, we need to make sure it's in the run list. We can accomplish this with the following command:

```
knife node run_list add db00 "role[base_server]"
knife node run_list add db00 "role[postgresql_server]"
```

After ensuring that your node has the base_server and postgresql_server roles added to the run list, you can run chef-client on the newly created host:

```
[jewart]% knife ssh 'name:db00' -x ubuntu 'sudo chef-client'
```

Once this is complete, assuming that everything went well, your new EC2 instance will have:

- PostgreSQL 9.3 server installed and running
- A new database (the name of which is defined from your configuration)
- A database user that is granted permission to connect
- Correct pg_hba.conf and postgresql.conf files for our service

Now that we have our database server configured, which can be verified by logging onto the server and ensuring that the service is running, let's take a look at setting up our web application.

Configuring the web server

In order for the web server to deploy the web app, we need to add the required roles to the web server, as we did with the database server:

```
knife node run_list add web00 "role[base_server]"
knife node run_list add web00 "role[web_server]"
```

Now, we can execute `chef-client` on the web host (again making sure to use `sudo` so that it has permission to do its work):

```
[jewart]% knife ssh 'name:web00' -x ubuntu 'sudo chef-client'
```

At this point, our web server will be in the following state:

- The following required packages will be installed:
  - Python 2.7 and development libraries
  - The PostgreSQL client development libraries
  - Git
- The directories our application needs to run are created
- A `virtualenv` tool, which is based on the system Python 2.7 is created
- Our application has been checked out from GitHub
- A configuration file in `/opt/webapp/src/config.py` is created by Chef
- Supervisord is configured to run our application and starts the `server.py` daemon

Now, you should be able to visit your newly installed web application at the following URL:

```
http://your-new-ec2-instance-hostname:8080
```

If you don't see your application, make sure that each of the preceding steps was successful.

Deploying your software

Deploying software should be treated just like your infrastructure; repeated deployments of the same commit and the same configuration should yield a consistent state of your environment. In this example, we will be able to deploy new updates to our web application simply by updating any nodes that use the `web_server` role. The combination of our recipe and our configuration data with the source code hosted in our GitHub repository will ensure that the most up-to-date configuration and source are placed on our host.

Manually deploying updates

Future deployments only require pushing changes to the master branch and then running `chef-client` on any web servers that are in the fleet. This can be accomplished on a single host (`web00`) using the following command:

```
knife ssh 'name:web00' -x ubuntu 'sudo chef-client'
```

This will tell `knife` that we want to SSH to the host whose name is `web00` as the `ubuntu` user (because that's the default EC2 user with `sudo` access) and execute `chef-client` as `root` via `sudo`. This will work well if we only have one host; however, as your capacity increases and you have multiple hosts, you will likely want to execute this on a group of hosts in the future. This can be accomplished using the search capability of Chef that allows you to expand a list of nodes that match a set of criteria. Here, we will want to build a list of all the hosts that have our `web_server` role associated with them. The following command will accomplish this:

```
knife ssh 'role:web_server' -x ubuntu 'sudo chef-client'
```

This will use Chef's search to find all nodes with the `web_server` role and then SSH to them sequentially, the same as before but only across multiple hosts instead of just one.

Automating deployment

The web application recipe is designed so that it syncs the source with the upstream GitHub repository. By doing this, we can execute the recipe multiple times, and any time there are updates, they will be pulled down onto the local host. If we wanted to, the process of deployments could be automated in the following fashion:

- Active development of the application happens in a separate, development branch
- Code is tested thoroughly and then merged into a master (or whatever branch is being deployed onto hosts) when it is stable and ready for production
- Hosts are configured to run `chef-client` on a fixed interval using a tool such as `cron` and will automatically update themselves

The possible issues with this are that bad code gets automatically deployed to endhosts and so on. However, with enough integration testing and a high enough confidence level, our code should be safe to deploy to production if it is in the master branch. Through a combination of tags and proper source management, rollbacks could be as simple as reverting the deploy branch to a known-good tag and they would happen as soon as the next `chef-client` execution or forced using `knife` as outlined previously.

Summary

A major attraction to Chef and infrastructure automation is the ability to deploy software and provision systems quickly and consistently. Using the cookbooks and examples outlined in this chapter, you should be able to model your application and its components, gather cookbooks required to deploy needed software, build cookbooks to configure and deploy custom software, and extend the examples to provide more functionalities or enhance your infrastructure.

Now that you have seen how to take an application from development to deployment, let's take a look at some more advanced examples of cookbook development, including writing custom providers and resources, working with secure data, searching Chef, and other ways of enhancing our recipes and cookbooks.

7
Beyond Basic Recipes and Cookbooks

So far, we have only really looked at how to use cookbooks as a consumer, not as a producer. In order to harness the true power of Chef, it is important to learn how to build our own cookbooks and recipes using the full feature set that Chef provides. This chapter covers:

- Advanced recipe concepts
- Managing your data using data bags
- Searching Chef from recipes
- Advanced scripting in recipes
- Authoring custom providers, resources, and definitions
- Dealing with encrypted data

Managing users

Basic user management in Chef is achieved through the use of the user resource. This resource allows you to add, remove, or otherwise manipulate users on your hosts. However, you can't possibly write recipes that contain one resource per user; it simply wouldn't scale. In order to make large-scale user management easier, we can combine some of Chef's capabilities such as data bags, per-role, per-node, and per-environment configuration to enable scalable user management.

Let's take a look at a user cookbook that can provide these abilities.

Evolution of a shell user recipe

First, let's take a look at a very naive user management recipe. This cookbook has a hardcoded `users` list; initially, it contains `frodo` and `samwise` and simply iterates through the list, creating users as it goes. Here is what the list may look like:

```ruby
users = [
  {
    'id' => 'frodo',
    'uid' => '100',
    'gid' => 100,
    'shell' => '/bin/hobbitshell',
    'comment' => 'Frodo of the nine fingers'
  }, {
    'id' => 'samwise',
    'uid' => '101',
    'gid' => 101,
    'shell' => '/bin/gardenshell',
    'comment' => 'Samwise the strong'
  }
]


users.each do |u|

  home_dir = "/home/#{u['id']}"

  user u['id'] do
    uid u['uid']
    gid u['gid']
    shell u['shell']
    comment u['comment']
    supports :manage_home => true
    home home_dir
  end

end
```

This approach will work for a handful of users, but it has the problem of being very limited in scope and difficult to maintain. It also isolates the list of users to this recipe, making it difficult to access data from other recipes and very brittle. The first thing we can improve is make the users accessible to this and any other recipe through the use of data bags. Let's take a look at how we can use data bags to make user data management simpler and more flexible.

Storing data in data bags

Data bags are designed to store arbitrary configuration data that pertains to your entire infrastructure. This may include users, global settings, firewall rules, and so on; if it can be modeled using basic JSON data structures such as arrays and dictionaries, it can be included in a data bag. We haven't touched much on these yet, so now is a good time to take a look at what they can do while modeling users.

Creating a data bag for users

Data bags are collections of data that are related to one another; for example, users, firewall rules, database servers, and so on. Here we will create a data bag that contains our user data. This is not intended to be a replacement for a directory service such as LDAP, though you could potentially use it to store all your user data and then write recipes to populate an LDAP server with user data (in this way, you may be able to keep an Active Directory system and a separate LDAP system in sync by making your Chef data bag the authoritative source for user data). Let's take a look at how to create and manipulate a data bag with user information:

```
[jewart]% knife data bag create users
Created data_bag[users]
```

Now, create a new user, frodo (you will need to have the EDITOR variable set to a text editor such as vim on Linux systems):

```
[jewart]% export EDITOR=vim
[jewart]% knife data bag create users frodo
Data bag users already exists
```

You will be presented with a new entity template that contains only one key, id, which is set to the name of the entity you created; in our case, frodo:

```
1 {
2   "id": "frodo",
3 }
```

Save this file and you will now have one, mostly empty, entity in your `users` data bag named `frodo`. You can check this with the `show` subcommand:

```
[jewart]% knife data bag show users
frodo
```

Every item in a data bag has to have a unique identifier, which can be meaningful or just a random identifier; in our case, it will double up as the login name for the user. We can take our previous data from the recipe and convert that to data bag elements by writing them to JSON files and uploading them with `knife`. To take advantage of uploads, we can create a directory, `users`, and create one JSON file per entry:

```
{
  "id" : "frodo",
  "uid" : "100",
  "gid" : 100,
  "shell" : "/bin/hobbitshell",
  "comment" : "Frodo of the nine fingers"
}


{
  "id" : "samwise",
  "uid" : "101",
  "gid" : 101,
  "shell" : "/bin/gardenshell",
  "comment" : "Samwise the strong"
}
```

Once you have created these, you should have two files, `frodo.json` and `samwise.json` inside a `users` directory. In order to bulk upload them, we use a `knife data bag` from the `<dir> <data bag name>` file in the following manner:

```
[jewart]% knife data bag from file users users
Updated data_bag_item[users::frodo]
Updated data_bag_item[users::samwise]
```

You can verify whether the entries were created correctly with the `knife data bag show <databag> <entity_id>` command:

```
[jewart]% knife data bag show users frodo
comment: Frodo of the nine fingers
gid:     100
```

```
id:      frodo
shell:   /bin/hobbitshell
uid:     100
```

Searching for data

Now that we have our data in a data bag in Chef, we can search for it using the search criteria. For example, if we wanted only all users whose names start with the letter *s*, we can search with the following command:

```
[jewart]% knife search users 'id:s*'
1 items found
```

```
chef_type:  data_bag_item
comment:    Samwise the strong
data_bag:   users
gid:        101
id:         samwise
shell:      /bin/gardenshell
uid:        101
```

Alternatively, if we wanted all the users in a given data bag, we can perform the following search:

```
[jewart]% knife search users 'id:*'
2 items found
```

```
chef_type:  data_bag_item
comment:    Frodo of the nine fingers
data_bag:   users
gid:        100
id:         frodo
shell:      /bin/hobbitshell
uid:        100
```

```
chef_type:  data_bag_item
comment:    Samwise the strong
```

```
data_bag:    users
gid:         101
id:          samwise
shell:       /bin/gardenshell
uid:         101
```

Searching inside recipes

Now that we have some data bag data created and can perform basic searches, let's see how we can use that to enhance our recipe using the built-in `search` method. This allows us to perform the searches we just ran with `knife` inside our recipes. The search method has a similar format to the `knife` command:

```
search(search_scope, search_criteria)
```

The following are some simple examples:

```
all_users = search(:users, 'id:*')
users_s = search(:users, 'id:s*')
all_nodes = search(:node, '*')
```

With this, we can enhance our shell user recipe to use the entities in the `users` data bag rather than hard code them. Our new recipe would look like the following:

```
# Replace the hard-coded users array with a search:
users = search(:users, 'id:*')

# Same as before, we've just moved our data source
users.each do |u|

  home_dir = "/home/#{u['id']}"

  user u['id'] do
    uid u['uid']
    gid u['gid']
    shell u['shell']
    comment u['comment']
    supports :manage_home => true
    home home_dir
  end

end
```

This is just a simple search; this will work for a small-scale infrastructure with a fixed set of users, where there's no need to restrict certain groups of users to certain hosts. You can easily imagine, however, a situation where some users are provisioned only to certain hosts through groups. Let's look at how we can achieve this with some better user metadata and a more advanced search.

Enhancing your user cookbook

In our previous example, we used the search method to find all of the users in our user's data bag. Here we will go one step further to isolate users based on arbitrary groups and see how we can limit the list of users to be provisioned using a combination of search, user metadata, and node configuration.

First, we need to add a `groups` key to our users. Let's add that to our existing user JSON data files and add a few more users, `legolas` and `gimli`:

```
{
  "id" : "frodo",
  "uid" : 100,
  "gid" : 100,
  "shell" : "/bin/hobbitshell",
  "comment" : "Frodo of the nine fingers",
  "groups" : ["hobbits", "fellowship"]
}

{
  "id" : "gimli",
  "uid" : 201,
  "gid" : 201,
  "shell" : "/bin/csh",
  "comment" : "Grumpy old dwarf",
  "groups" : [ "dwarves", "fellowship" ]
}

{
  "id" : "legolas",
  "uid" : 200,
  "gid" : 200,
  "shell" : "/bin/zsh",
  "comment" : "Keen eyed Legolas",
  "groups" : [ "elves", "fellowship" ]
}

{
```

```
    "id" : "samwise",
    "uid" : "101",
    "gid" : 101,
    "shell" : "/bin/gardenshell",
    "comment" : "Samwise the strong",
    "groups" : ["hobbits", "fellowship"]
}
```

Once again, we update the existing records and create our new records using `knife data bag from file`:

```
[jewart]% knife data bag from file users users
Updated data_bag_item[users::frodo]
Updated data_bag_item[users::gimli]
Updated data_bag_item[users::legolas]
Updated data_bag_item[users::samwise]
```

Now that you have a few additional users in your data bag, and each user has some group metadata attached to it, let's take a look at how we can use this to provision only certain users on specific hosts. First, we need to be able to limit our search scope dynamically; otherwise, we will need to modify our recipe on a per-host basis and that just won't scale. We need to add a dynamic search query to our recipe with something like the following code:

```
search_criteria = "groups:#{node[:shell_users][:group]}"
```

This creates a search criteria string that will match objects that have the value specified somewhere in their `groups` key. In order to make this dynamic per host, we will store this value in a `shell_users` hash under the `group` key. For example, if you wanted to add all users that are in the `hobbits` group to a specific node, then your node's configuration would need to contain the following:

```
{
  "shell_users": {
    "group": "hobbits",
  }
}
```

This will build a search criteria of `"groups" : "hobbits"`, which if we pass to the `search` method will yield all entries in the `users` data bag that have `"hobbits"` inside their groups list. Consider the following recipe code:

```
users = search(:users, search_criteria)
```

The node configuration data will expand the search criteria during an execution on this node to be the following:

```
search_criteria = "groups:hobbits"
```

Given the data we have stored in our users data bag, this would match `samwise` and `frodo` as they have the hobbits group in their groups list. We can verify this by trying the same search on the command line with `knife`:

```
[jewart]% knife search users "groups:hobbits"
2 items found


chef_type: data_bag_item
comment:   Frodo of the nine fingers
data_bag:  users
gid:       100
groups:
  hobbits
  fellowship
id:        frodo
shell:     /bin/hobbitshell
uid:       100


chef_type: data_bag_item
comment:   Samwise the strong
data_bag:  users
gid:       101
groups:
  hobbits
  fellowship
id:        samwise
shell:     /bin/gardenshell
uid:       101
```

As you can see, this allows us to narrowly define the list of users to be managed through the combination of entity metadata and dynamic search criteria. You can build more advanced applications using this methodology with more advanced search criteria and incorporating more of the entities' metadata.

Distributing SSH keys

In addition to managing user accounts, we can also use Chef to manage SSH keys. Because a given user's accepted SSH keys are stored in a per-user configuration file, it is quite simple to manipulate them. By creating a template for SSH-authorized keys, we can build a recipe that will take the SSH key data from the data bag and populate the authorized keys file on the host. By doing this, users' SSH keys can be stored in Chef and distributed to any number of hosts with just one command. This solves the problems typically associated with distribution and revocation of SSH keys inside an organization.

Templating the authorized keys

Here is a sample template we will use for our user's authorized keys file; this would be defined in an `authorized_keys.erb` file:

```
<% if @ssh_keys.is_a?(Array) %>
<%= @ssh_keys.join("\n") %>
<% else %>
<%= @ssh_keys %>
<% end %>
```

This is a very simple template that has only two cases: if the template variable `ssh_keys` is an array, it will print them out with a new line in between them; otherwise, it will simply print out the contents of the variable.

To use this template, we will simply provide it with a list of SSH-compatible key strings:

```
template "#{home_dir}/.ssh/authorized_keys" do
  source "authorized_keys.erb"
  owner u['id']
  group u['gid'] || u['id']
  mode "0600"
  variables :ssh_keys => u['ssh_keys']
end
```

Now, we can modify one of our previous user JSON entities to add SSH keys:

```
{
  "id" : "frodo",
  "uid" : 100,
  "gid" : 100,
  "shell" : "/bin/hobbitshell",
  "comment" : "Frodo of the nine fingers",
  "groups" : ["hobbits", "fellowship"],
```

```
    "ssh_keys": [
        "ssh-dss RG9uJ3Qgd29ycnksIFNhbS4gUm9zaWUga25vd3MgYW4gaWRpb3Q
gd2hlbiBzaGUgc2VlcyBvbmUu frodo@shire",
        "ssh-dss TXkgbWFzdGVyLCBTYXVyb24gdGhlIEdyZWF0LCBiaWRzIHRoZWUgd
2VsY29tZS4gSXMgdGhlcmUgYW55IGluIHRoaXMgcm91dCB3aXRoIGF1dGhvcml0eSB0
byB0cmVhdCB3aXRoIG1lPyA= sauron@mordor"
    ]
}
```

```
% knife data bag from file users ssh_keys/frodo.json
Updated data_bag_item[users::frodo]
```

Once your user has been updated, check whether your newly added metadata has been updated, looking for your new ssh_keys key in the entity. In order to do that, you can show the contents of your data bag using the following command:

```
% knife data bag show users frodo
```

The output of this should line up with your newly updated JSON content. With these added, we can write a new recipe that will allow us to deploy authorized_keys files for each user on our hosts. Our recipe will use the same search criteria from our previous recipe as we want to apply our SSH keys to all of our shell users.

This recipe is responsible for making sure that the proper directory for SSH is created and has the correct permissions, as well as creating the authorized_keys file with the necessary permissions and storing the SSH keys associated with the user in /home/user/.ssh/authorized_keys:

```ruby
search_criteria = "groups:#{node[:shell_users][:group]}"

search(:users, search_criteria) do |u|

  home_dir = "/home/#{u['id']}"

  directory "#{home_dir}/.ssh" do
    owner u['id']
    group u['gid']
    mode "0700"
    recursive true
  end

  template "#{home_dir}/.ssh/authorized_keys" do
    source "authorized_keys.erb"
    owner u['id']
    group u['gid']
```

```
    mode "0600"
    variables :ssh_keys => u['ssh_keys']
  end

end
```

Adding deployment keys

If you have ever deployed a Rails application to hosts that need to have access to your source code in a GitHub or BitBucket repository, then you will know how handy it is to manage deployment keys across a fleet of hosts. We can easily generate a recipe that looks at a node's list of deployment users following our previous examples as a starting point. Here, we look for **deploy users** instead of shell users, as these are the ones we want to manage deployment keys for. Note that in this example, these users would also need to be included in the shell_users group to ensure that they get created by our previous recipe:

```
search_criteria = "groups:#{node[:deploy_users][:group]}"

search(:users, search_criteria) do |u|
  home_dir = "/home/#{u['id']}"

  directory "#{home_dir}/.ssh" do
    owner u['id']
    group u['gid'] || u['id']
    mode "0700"
    recursive true
  end

  template "#{home_dir}/.ssh/id_rsa" do
    source "deploy_key.erb"
    owner u['id']
    group u['gid'] || u['id']
    mode "0600"
    variables :key => u['deploy_key']
  end
end
```

To use this new recipe, the deployment users would need to be modified to include a group identifier and their private key. The group would be reserved for users involved in deploying your application and be added to the user's groups key in Chef. Additionally, an unencrypted SSH private key would need to be present in a deploy_key field.

Including unencrypted SSH keys can pose a security risk. This can be mitigated using encrypted data bags or an external security material management service.

Writing custom extensions

With Chef, you are given immediate access to a number of resources: files, users, packages, templates, and so on. However, there will always be times when this does not provide you with everything that you need. Fortunately, the built-in Chef resources or LWRPs (light-weight resource providers) are just Ruby code and were built with the intention of providing a framework for end users to build their own components. This means that you can easily build your own custom resources, and these can be shared with others just like any built-in LWRP.

Developing a custom definition

One of the simplest resources that we can build is a **definition**—a definition is like a resource with only one built-in provider. These can be thought of as reusable modules that you can leverage inside of your recipes. If you find yourself writing the same thing *repeatedly* in your recipes, then it is probably a good candidate to write a custom definition. For example, let's look at how we can build two different definitions: one for executing Python's PIP, the Python package installation tool, to install the contents of a `requirements.txt` file for a Python application, and another to install applications that follow the same pattern.

Organizing your code

As discussed before, cookbooks can have a definitions directory inside them. The contents of this directory are included in your cookbook runs and should have one per definition. For our PIP resource, we will create a file, `definitions/pip_requirements.rb`, and for our application template, `definitions/python_web_application.rb`. These will each contain the respective definitions.

Writing a definition for using PIP

Definitions look like any Chef component—they are composed of resources, variables, scripts, and anything else you use in a recipe. However, unlike a recipe, they are designed to be reused. Where a recipe is designed with a specific effect in mind such as deploying a specific application, the definition is designed to be consumed by recipes to reduce duplicate code.

Each definition is encapsulated in a `define` block, a no-op version, or our PIP example would look like this:

```
define :pip_requirements do
end
```

This example does absolutely nothing, but it can be used in a recipe as follows:

```
pip_requirements "app_requirements" do
end
```

Just in the same way you would use a file, `user`, or template block in your recipe, you can use your custom definitions. Now, let's enhance our definition by using the `name` parameter—the string argument passed to the `pip_requirements` block in your recipe; here, it is `app_requirements`:

```
define :pip_requirements , :action => :skip do
  name = params[:name]
end
```

Each invocation of a definition passes the parameters in the block to the definition; these are accessed inside the definition through the `params` hash. There is one special parameter, `:name`, which can come from the first argument before the block, as shown in the previous code, or from the name parameter inside the block. This is a convenience parameter designed to make recipes more readable by allowing the developer to write:

```
resource "some handy description" do
...
end
```

This code is easier to read than:

```
resource do
  name "some handy description"
end
```

Given this information, let's look at the PIP example from `pip_requirements.rb`:

```
define :pip_requirements , :action => :skip do
    name = params[:name]
    requirements_file = params[:requirements_file]
    pip = params[:pip]
    user = params[:user]
    group = params[:group]

    if params[:action] == :run
```

```
        script "pip_install_#{name}" do
          interpreter "bash"
          user "#{user}"
          group "#{group}"
          code <<-EOH
          #{pip} install -r #{requirements_file}
          EOH
          only_if { File.exists?("#{requirements_file}") and File.
exists?("#{pip}") }
        end
    end
end
```

Here, the definition expects five arguments: the resource name, the path to the requirements.txt file, the pip binary to use, as well as the user and group to execute pip as. The reason that the resource accepts the path to pip is to allow using pip inside a Python virtual environment. By doing this, the definition becomes a little more flexible in situations where you need to install your requirements into a different location on the system.

Also note that we can define default parameters as part of the definition's signature:

```
define :pip_requirements , :action => :skip do
```

In this case, the default action is :skip, but it can be set to anything you want it to be. Here it is set to :skip so that it only gets invoked deliberately rather than by virtue of being used in a recipe.

As this is a simple definition, it only contains one resource — a script block that will effectively execute pip install -r /path/to/requirements.txt as the specified user and group. An example use of this definition can be seen as follows:

```
pip_requirements "requirements" do
  action :run
  pip "/usr/local/bin/pip"
  user node[:app][:user]
  group node[:app][:group]
  requirements_file "#{app_root}/src/requirements.txt"
end
```

This can be used in place of the built-in script resource:

```
script "pip_install_#{name}" do
  interpreter "bash"
  user node[:app][:user]
  group node[:app][:group]
  code <<-EOH
```

```
  /usr/local/bin/pip install -r #{app_root}/src/requirements.txt
EOH
only_if {
  File.exists?("#{app_root}/src/requirements.txt") and
  File.exists?("/usr/local/bin/pip")
}
end
```

Following Chef's declarative language, building definitions such as this one makes it more obvious as to what is happening, rather than how it is happening. We have abstracted the shell script and guard tests behind a façade, that is the `pip_requirements` definition, which is more clear in its effect when you read a recipe; you don't need to examine the contents of the `script` block to deduce what is happening as the resource name tells you exactly what's going to be done.

Defining a full application template

If you have applications that follow the same structure (think applications that use a common framework such as Rails, Django, Pyramids, Python-tornado, and so on), then you would likely want to define a common definition for what such an application looks like. Consider here a definition to install a Python web application from GitHub using some common idioms:

```
define :tornado_application do
  app_name = params[:name]
  app_root = params[:app_root]
  app_user = params[:user]
  app_group = params[:group]

  python_interpreter = params[:python_interpreter] ||
                       "/usr/bin/python3.3"
  github_repo = params[:github_repo]
  deploy_branch = params[:deploy_branch] || "deploy"

  virtualenv = "#{app_root}/python"
  virtual_python = "#{virtualenv}/bin/python"
  app_dir = "#{app_root}/src/#{app_name}"

  # Need to install SSH key for GitHub
  # this comes from the ssh_known_hosts cookbook
  ssh_known_hosts_entry 'github.com'

  # Base package requirements
  package "git"
```

```
package "libpq-dev"
package "libxml2-dev"
package "python3.3"
package "python3.3-dev"

directory "#{app_root}" do
  owner "#{app_user}"
  group "#{app_group}"
  mode "0755"
  action :create
  recursive true
end

# Create directories
["bin", "src", "logs", "conf", "tmp"].each do |child_dir|
  directory "#{app_root}/#{child_dir}" do
    owner "#{app_user}"
    group "#{app_group}"
    mode "0755"
    action :create
    recursive true
  end
end


# Install Python virtualenv
python_virtualenv "#{virtualenv}" do
  owner "#{app_user}"
  group "#{app_group}"
  action :create
  interpreter "#{python_interpreter}"
end

# Application checkout
git "#{app_dir}" do
  repository "#{github_repo}"
  action :sync
  user "#{app_user}"
  branch "#{deploy_branch}"
end

# Python dependencies for app
pip_requirements "tornado_app[#{app_name}]" do
  action :run
```

```
      pip "#{virtualenv}/bin/pip"
      user "#{app_user}"
      group "#{app_group}"
      requirements_file "#{app_dir}/requirements.txt"
    end

  end
```

This definition can be used as shown in the following example:

```
tornado_application "image_resizer" do
  app_root "/opt/webapps"
  user "webapp"
  group "webapp"
  deploy_branch "master"
  github_repo "git@github.com:myorg/image_resizer.git"
  python_interpreter "/usr/bin/python3.3"
end
```

According to the previous definition, this would do the following:

- Add a system-wide SSH-known key for `github.com` (required to perform a Git clone and guarantees that future key changes will work)
- Install any required packages if they didn't already exist, including Git, Python, and the `postgresql` client
- Ensure any application-required directories exist for data such as binaries, logs, configuration, and more
- Create a Python virtual environment based on the supplied Python interpreter (3.3) in `<app_root>/python`
- Clone or sync (if it was already cloned) the source code from `<github_repo>` to `<app_root>/src/<app_name>`
- Install the requirements specified in `<app_root>/src/<app_name>/requirements.txt` using the copy of `pip` from the virtual environment in `<app_root>/python`

Assuming you had another similarly structured application, but you wanted to use a different user, group, Python interpreter, and deployment branch, you can easily configure it using the following resource:

```
tornado_application "restful_api" do
  app_root "/opt/webapps"
  user "restapi"
  group "restapi"
  deploy_branch "production"
```

```
    github_repo "git@github.com:myorg/restful_api.git"
    python_interpreter "/usr/bin/python3.2"
  end
```

As you can see, definitions allow us to define reusable resources in Chef. There are three primary benefits to this approach:

- Simplified recipes are easier to read, have clearer intentions, and less code to audit, which makes them less error prone

- Any changes to the definition are automatically applied to any usage of the definition, which means you don't need to maintain multiple variations

- It's easier to test because it's designed to be parameterized and modular

Now that you see how easy it is to write custom resources for Chef through definitions, let's examine writing a full-blown resource that has a separate provider implementation.

Building a resource

A Chef LWRP is composed of two primary components, a **resource** and a **provider**. The resource is the blueprint for what is being provided; it describes the resource, including what actions can be taken by a resource, the properties that describe the resource, and any other high-level information about it. The provider is responsible for the actual implementation of the resource. In programming terms, the resource is an abstract class or interface where the provider is a concrete class or implementation. For example, one of Chef's built-in resources is the package resource; however, this is a very high-level resource. The package resource describes what a package is and what a package can do but not how to manage them. That work is left to the providers, including RPM, APT, FreeBSD packages, and other backend systems that are capable of managing on-disk installation of packages.

Defining the resource

As an example, let's take a look at an S3 bucket resource:

```
actions :sync
default_action :sync if defined?(default_action) # Chef > 10.8

# Default action for Chef <= 10.8
def initialize(*args)
  super
  @action = :sync
```

```
end

# Target folder on the host to sync with the S3 bucket
attribute :destination, :kind_of => String,
          :name_attribute => true
# Anything to skip when syncing
attribute :omit, :kind_of => Array
# AWS Access / secret key
attribute :access_key_id, :kind_of => String
attribute :secret_access_key, :kind_of => String
```

Here, our resource is an S3 bucket that declares the actions it can take along with the attributes that it relies on. Here, our resource declares that it has one available action, sync, which is the default action and that it has four attributes: the destination, what files to skip, the access key, and the secret key.

Implementing the provider

The provider is where the logic for the resource is placed—it is responsible for acting on the resource being described. For our S3 bucket, it looks like the following:

```
require 'chef/mixin/language'

# Only run as needed
def whyrun_supported?
  true
end

action :sync do
 Chef::Log.debug("Checking #{new_resource} for changes")
 fetch_from_s3(new_resource.source) do |raw_file|
   Chef::Log.debug "copying remote file from origin #{raw_file.path}
to destination #{new_resource.destination}"
   FileUtils.cp raw_file.path, new_resource.destination
 end

 new_resource.updated_by_last_action(true)
end

def load_current_resource
  chef_gem 'aws-sdk' do
    action :install
```

```
    end

    require 'aws/s3'

    current_resource = new_resource.destination
    current_resource
  end

  def fetch_from_s3(source)
    begin
      protocol, bucket = URI.split(source).compact
      AWS::S3::Base.establish_connection!(
          :access_key_id     => new_resource.access_key_id,
          :secret_access_key => new_resource.secret_access_key
      )

      bucket.objects.each do |obj|
        name = obj.key

        if !new_resource.skip.contains(name)
          Chef::Log.debug("Downloading #{name} from S3 bucket
#{bucket}")
          obj = AWS::S3::S3Object.find name, bucket

          file = Tempfile.new("chef-s3-file")
          file.write obj.value
          Chef::Log.debug("File #{name} is #{file.size} bytes on disk")
          begin
            yield file
          ensure
            file.close
          end
        else
          Chef::Log.debug("Skipping #{name} because it's in the skip
list")
        end
      end

    rescue URI::InvalidURIError
      Chef::Log.warn("Expected an S3 URL but found #{source}")
      nil
    end
  end
```

Let's take a look at the provider, piece by piece. The first thing the provider does, beyond including any required libraries, is to inform Chef that it supports **why-run**. This is a mechanism that Chef provides so that resources can be more easily tested by effectively not wiring a resource to a provider. This allows developers to test their resources, in what is effectively a **dry-run** mode, before running them live against a system:

```
# Only run as needed
def whyrun_supported?
  true
end
```

Next, there is an `action` block—this registers the provided block as the logic to be executed for the specified action (in this case, `:sync`). This has the general form such as:

```
action :<action name> do
  # Real work in here
end
```

In this case, the only supported action is sync, and so there is only one `action` block:

```
action :sync do
 Chef::Log.debug("Checking #{new_resource} for changes")
 fetch_from_s3(new_resource.source) do |raw_file|
   Chef::Log.debug "copying remote file from origin #{raw_file.path}
to destination #{new_resource.destination}"
   FileUtils.cp raw_file.path, new_resource.destination
 end
 new_resource.updated
end
```

Here, the `:sync` action leverages the `fetch_from_s3` method, which yields a local copy of a file in the remote bucket once it has been downloaded. Then, the file is copied from the temporary location locally into the specified destination.

Modifying resources

Inside of this action, you will notice that there is an actor, `new_resource` (which is actually a built-in method). This describes what the state of the named resource should be when the provider has completed its execution for the specified resource; this may or may not differ from the current state of the resource on the node. In the case of an initial run, `new_resource` will almost certainly be different from `current_resource`, but that may not always be the case on subsequent runs.

As an example, if we have a recipe with the following S3 bucket resource declared:

```
s3_bucket "s3://mychefbucket/.resource" do
  action :sync
  skip ["foo.txt", "bar.txt]
  destination "/opt/app_data"
  access_key_id node[:app][:aws_access_key]
  secret_access_key node[:app][:aws_secret_key]
  owner node[:app][:user]
  group node[:app][:group]
  mode "0755"
end
```

Then, the `new_resource` actor would have its member variables populated with the parameters passed to the `s3_bucket` resource. Again, this is the expected state of the resource, the way it should be when the execution by the provider is complete. In this case, when the provider code is executed, `new_resource.destination` will be "/opt/app_data" and `new_resource.skip` will be a list of "foo.txt" and "bar.txt" and so on. This allows you to pass data into the instance of the resource in the same way that was possible with the PIP and Tornado application definitions.

Loading an existing resource

One thing that is less obvious about the provider script is the `load_current_resource` method that is not called from within the provider. This method is used by Chef to find a resource on the node based on the attributes that are provided by the recipe. This is useful to determine if anything needs to be done to bring an existing resource on the host such as a file, a user account, or a directory of files, up to date with the data that is provided during execution of the recipe.

It might make sense to extend this provider to precompute the hashes of the files that already exist in the directory on-disk as specified by `destination`. This way, the provider can be updated to only download any remote files in S3 that have a different fingerprint than a similarly named resource on disk. This prevents unnecessary work from being performed, which saves time, bandwidth, and other resources.

Here, however, it is also used to ensure that any dependencies to download files are installed; in this case, the AWS gem is required to use the S3 client. This works because the `load_current_resource` method gets called on early to determine the current state of the resource. If the resources are the same, then the provider has nothing to do. The current implementation just clobbers whatever files are local with the contents of the S3 bucket (more of a one-way download than a sync, really).

Declaring that a resource was updated

Resources have a built-in method, `updated_by_last_action`, which is called inside the `:sync` action all the time in this example. This method notifies the resource that the node was updated successfully. This should only be set to `true` if everything was successfully updated; failures should not make this call unless they set it to `false`. It is useful to know what resources have been updated for reporting or other purposes. For example, you can use this flag to identify what resources have been updated:

```
module SimpleReport
  class UpdatedResources < Chef::Handler
    def report
      Chef::Log.info "Resources updated this run:"
      run_status.updated_resources.each do |r|
          Chef::Log.info "  #{r.to_s}"
      end
    end
  end
end
```

Working with data bags

There are a number of things you can do with data bags.

Securing your data bags

Data bags are just JSON data, but they are stored in the system as plain text, without any security. They are also downloaded onto various hosts throughout the life cycle, which can lead to leaking of potentially sensitive information. Fortunately, Chef has a method that lets you secure this data by using `knife`, along with secret keys to keep data in data bags encrypted.

Secret keys

Encrypting a data bag item requires a secret key; one way of generating a secret key is to generate a random number and use the **Base64** encoding of that number as the secret key. This should have any line endings removed to ensure it works properly on all platforms, regardless of platform-specific line endings. Here is a quick way to generate one using the `openssl` command line tool combined with `tr` to remove any line endings:

```
$ openssl rand -base64 512 | tr -d '\r\n' > ~/.chef/data_bag_secret
```

Encrypting your data

In order to encrypt your data bag item, you must use `knife` and pass the `--secret` or `--secret-file` flags to `knife` when creating the item. For example, to create a data bag called `credentials` and store a new entry, `aws`, inside it, you would use the following command (make sure you set your EDITOR environment variable first):

```
$ knife data bag create credentials aws --secret-file ~/.chef/data_bag_
secret
```

As mentioned before, you will be presented with the contents of your new data bag item in your editor, unencrypted:

```
1 {
2   "id": "aws", ·
3 }
```

Here, we can add some properties, such as a secret key:

```
1 {
2   "id": "aws", ·
3   "secret_key": "A21AbFdeccFB213f"
4 }
```

Once you save this, `knife` will tell you that the new data bag was created, along with the new data bag item in Chef, just as it did with the user data earlier. The only difference will be that this time the data stored in the Chef server has been encrypted using the symmetric key you provided:

```
$ knife data bag create credentials aws --secret-file ~/.chef/data_bag_
secret
Created data_bag[credentials]
Created data_bag_item[aws]
```

To check whether your newly created data bag entry was encrypted, use `knife`, as we have before, to show the contents of an item:

```
$ knife data bag show credentials aws

id:          aws
secret_key:
  cipher:         aes-256-cbc
  encrypted_data:
```

```
SG4z4jd4VAnJ4gG0wPcJWOX7H+ZNSxG5PH+n7EgHFV9e1SciVznjaAbzK61c
EW0/
iv:        rKB0riCr84QhBkw+Wgc/5Q==
version:   1
```

Decrypting your data

In order to decrypt the data in the data bag item, you need to provide the same symmetric key as you provided when you encrypted it, using the `--secret` or `--secret-file` argument, as can be seen here:

```
$ knife data bag show credentials aws --secret-file ~/.chef/data_bag_
secret
id:        aws
secret_key: A21AbFdeccFB213f
```

If it wasn't already obvious to you, make certain you do not lose this file. Without your secret key or secret file, you will not be able to decrypt the data in your data bag. It may be worth encrypting the secret file with a passphrase if you are going to be transmitting it to nontrusted locations as well.

Storing keys on nodes

An encryption key can also be stored in an alternate file on the nodes that need it, and you can specify the path location to the file inside an attribute; however, `EncryptedDataBagItem.load` expects to see the actual secret as the third argument rather than a path to the secret file. In this case, you can use `EncryptedDataBagItem.load_secret` to slurp the secret file contents and then pass them:

```
# inside your attribute file:
default[:app][:aws_creds_secret] = "/opt/secret/aws.secret"

# Inside your recipe
aws_secret = Chef::EncryptedDataBagItem.load_secret
        "#{node[:app][: aws_creds_secret]}"

aws_creds = Chef::EncryptedDataBagItem.load
            "credentials", "aws", aws_secret

aws_creds["secret_key"]
```

Searching your data

As we discussed earlier, you can search through your data bags using Boolean search logic. This permits you to find only the entries in your data bags that you need. The same search query language is used on the command line with `knife` as it is in your recipes, so that you can test your queries on the command line to ensure that they produce the right results before you put them in your recipes. You can also search through other resources as well, not just data bags.

Searching your data bags with knife

The `knife` tool uses the `search` command to search through your data bags. The general syntax is:

```
knife search <source> "<search criteria>"
```

Searching your data bags from a recipe

Inside a recipe, the `search` method is used to search through a data bag. The syntax for this is:

```
search(:source, "search criteria")
```

Querying your data

The search query format is reasonably straightforward and looks like most other search engines that support the Boolean logic.

Searches on attributes come in the form of `key:value`; so for example, if you wanted to find all of the users who were dwarves from our earlier data sets, you can use the search query:

```
knife search users "groups:dwarves"
```

Negating a search term can be accomplished by placing NOT in front of the search term. For example, all users who are not hobbits will be:

```
knife search users "NOT groups:hobbits"
```

You can also use an OR modifier:

```
knife search users "groups:elves OR groups:hobbits"
```

This last search criteria would yield the users `legolas`, `samwise`, and `frodo` as Frodo and Samwise are in the group called hobbits and Legolas is in the elves group.

While combining search terms, you can logically AND them together as well. For example, all users with a GID starting with 20, who contain the group elves can be found using the following query:

```
knife search users "groups:elves AND gid:20*"
```

You can search your nodes with the same query language—in order to find all nodes that are running some form of windows, you can search for the platform being anything that starts with win:

```
knife search node "platform:win*"
```

This will yield all Windows hosts (results have been shortened a bit):

```
4 items found


Node Name:    i-13d0bd4f
Roles:
Platform:     windows 6.2.9200


Node Name:    WIN-CJDQ9DEOJFK
Roles:        umbraco_cms
Platform:     windows 6.2.9200


Node Name:    00c0ff3300
Roles:
Platform:     windows 6.2.9200


Node Name:    rs-5889646228538071
Roles:
Platform:     windows 6.2.9200
```

Or, you can search for all nodes that are running windows and contain the role umbraco_cms:

```
knife search node "platform:win* AND role:umbraco_cms"
```

Or, if you wanted to eliminate those nodes that run the Umbraco CMS, you can easily invert the role condition:

```
knife search node "platform:win* AND NOT role:umbraco_cms"
```

Because Chef uses Apache Solr to search its data, you can refer to the Apache Solr documentation on building more advanced query logic at `http://wiki.apache.org/solr/SolrQuerySyntax`.

Managing multiple machines with search queries

The search criteria can be used for all sorts of places: in recipes, on the command line, through API calls, and more. One very interesting application is being able to use the search query to SSH to multiple machines to perform commands in parallel:

```
knife ssh "fqdn:*.east.mycorp.com AND platform:ubuntu" "chef-client" -x
app_user
```

This will contact the Chef server and ask for the nodes that match the given query string (machines whose FQDN matches the wildcard expression `"*.east.mycorp.com"` and that are running Ubuntu) and then connect to them via SSH as the user `app_user` and run the `chef-client` command on each of them. Again, you can restrict (or expand) the server list by using a more (or less) specific query.

Once you have mastered this aspect of using `knife`, you can learn more about its support for executing multiple connections concurrently and even interact with terminal multiplexers such as `screen` and `tmux`.

Summary

Chef has lots of mechanisms to build advanced automation, including building your own definitions, resources, and providers, as well as storing and accessing complex configuration data and even securely encrypting it. This chapter has shown you how to manage data in data bags (including encrypted data), use Chef's advanced search engine to find and manipulate data in your system from the command line and in recipes, as well as develop definitions for reusable recipe development, and even build custom resources and providers for use in your cookbooks.

In the next chapter, we will cover some more advanced ways to use Chef, including interacting with the Chef shell, automation and integration with Chef using scripts and APIs, external tools and resources, advanced testing including integration testing, and using Chef-solo and Vagrant to manage your development environments.

8

Extras You Need to Know

This chapter will cover how to use Chef to build custom bootstrap scripts for systems, enhanced command-line tool concepts, leverage Chef for automation, integration, and securely store sensitive data in the system. Some topics that will be covered in this chapter include:

- Using Chef-solo with Vagrant
- Interacting with the Chef shell
- Debugging recipes
- Advanced command-line usage
- Automating and integrating with Chef
- More testing methodologies

Vagrant and Chef-solo

Vagrant is a very useful tool to build development environments, where it provides tools to build virtual machines that contain everything you need to get started with building software. Consider, for a moment, working on a team that builds software and relies on a **service-oriented architecture (SOA)**, and this software is composed of a number of different services. In order for it to work, you may be required to install and configure all of the dependent services to even begin working on a part of the system; this could be a time-consuming and error-prone exercise for even seasoned developers. Now imagine that all you had to do was download a configuration file and execute vagrant to do it for you—this is the world of Vagrant.

One of the interesting facets of Vagrant is that it has support to provision new instances using a number of different mechanisms. Currently, this list includes 10 or so different tools, but the most interesting two are Chef-solo and Chef client. By now, you should be comfortable with how you might provision a virtual machine using the Chef client; it's not much different than provisioning an EC2 instance or a dedicated server. However, we haven't discussed using Chef-solo much yet, so this is a good time to learn more about it.

Installing Vagrant

Historically, Vagrant was installed via RubyGems; this is no longer the case, and if you have an older version installed as a gem, it is recommended that you remove it before installing Vagrant. Installers for all supported platforms (OS X, Windows, and Linux) are available at the following URL:

```
http://www.vagrantup.com/downloads
```

If you are new to Vagrant, then in addition to installing Vagrant, you will want to install VirtualBox for simplicity, as Vagrant has built-in support for VirtualBox. Vagrant does support other providers such as VMWare and AWS, but it requires plugins that are not distributed with the core Vagrant installation in order for them to work.

Once you have installed Vagrant and VirtualBox, then you can continue on with the following examples.

Provisioning a new host with Vagrant

Provisioning a new virtual instance requires that you build a Vagrant configuration file called `Vagrantfile`. This file serves two purposes: to denote that the directory is a Vagrant project (similar to how a `Makefile` indicates a project that is built with Make), and to describe the virtual machine that is being run, including how to provision it, what operating system to use, where to find the virtual image, and so on. Because this is just a plain text file, you can include it along with any auxiliary files required to build the image such as cookbooks, recipes, JSON files, installers, and so on, and commit it to the source control for others to use.

In order to begin, you will want to create a directory that will house your new Vagrant project. On Unix-like systems, we would bootstrap our project similarly to the following command:

```
mkdir -p ~/vagrant/chef_solo
cd ~/vagrant/chef_solo
```

Windows hosts will be the same except for different paths and changes in methods of directory creation. Once this step is complete, you will need to create a skeleton configuration located in `~/vagrant/chef_solo/Vagrantfile`. This file can be generated using `vagrant init`, but we would not want to use the contents of the generated file; so, we will skip that step and manually construct our `Vagrantfile` instead (with a simple one-line configuration that uses a base image of Ubuntu 13.10). Your `Vagrantfile` should look like the following code:

```
Vagrant.configure("2") do |config|
    config.vm.box = "ubuntu/trusty64"
end
```

Here, `"2"` is the API version, which is currently Version 2.0 as of this writing, and the configured base image (or `box`) is the Ubuntu Trusty (14.04) 64-bit image. Before you use this base image, it needs to be downloaded to your local machine; you can add it to Vagrant using the `box add` command:

vagrant box add ubuntu/trusty64

> This step will take a few minutes on a fast connection, so be prepared to wait while this completes if you are following along interactively. Also note that if you skip this step, the base image will automatically be downloaded while running `vagrant up` to start your virtual machine.

For future references, if you want to find alternative OS images to use for your Vagrant machines, you should look at Vagrant Cloud (`https://vagrantcloud.com/`), where you can find a number of other freely available base images to download for use with Vagrant.

Booting your Vagrant image

Once your base image has completed downloading, you will use the `vagrant up` command to boot up a new virtual machine. By doing this, you will instruct Vagrant to read the `Vagrantfile` and boot a new instance of the base image:

```
Bringing machine 'default' up with 'virtualbox' provider...
==> default: Importing base box 'ubuntu/trusty64'...
==> default: Matching MAC address for NAT networking...
==> default: Checking if box 'ubuntu/trusty64' is up to date...
==> default: Setting the name of the VM: chef_solo_
default_1402875519251_51266
==> default: Clearing any previously set forwarded ports...
==> default: Clearing any previously set network interfaces...
```

```
==> default: Preparing network interfaces based on configuration...
    default: Adapter 1: nat
==> default: Forwarding ports...
    default: 22 => 2222 (adapter 1)
==> default: Booting VM...
==> default: Waiting for machine to boot. This may take a few
minutes...
    default: SSH address: 127.0.0.1:2222
    default: SSH username: vagrant
    default: SSH auth method: private key
    default: Warning: Connection timeout. Retrying...
==> default: Machine booted and ready!
==> default: Checking for guest additions in VM...
==> default: Mounting shared folders...
    default: /vagrant => /Users/jewart/Temp/vagrant/chef_solo
```

As you can see from the output, Vagrant performed the following things:

- Used the base image `ubuntu/trusty64`
- Configured VirtualBox to use a NAT adapter, mapping port `22` to `2222`
- Started the VM in headless mode (such that you don't see the VirtualBox GUI)
- Created a user, `vagrant`, with a private key for authentication
- Mounted a shared folder mapping `/vagrant` on the guest to the Vagrant workspace on the host

Now that you have a running guest, you can control it by running vagrant commands from inside of the vagrant workspace (`~/vagrant/chef_solo`); for example, you can SSH into it using the following command:

vagrant ssh

And you can destroy the running instance with the following command:

vagrant destroy

Go ahead and SSH into your new guest and poke around a little bit—you will notice that it looks just like any other Ubuntu 14.04 host. Once you are done, use `destroy` to destroy it so that you can look at how to provision your Vagrant image using Chef-solo. It's important to know that if you use `destroy` on your guest, changes to your Vagrant image are not persisted; so, any changes you have made inside it will not be saved and will not exist the next time you use `vagrant up` to start the VM.

Combining Vagrant with Chef-solo

In our previous example, our `Vagrantfile` simply declared that our guest relied on the `ubuntu/trusty64` image as the base image via the `config.vm.box` property. Next, we will look at how to extend our configuration file to use the Chef-solo provisioner to install some software on our guest host. Here, we will use Chef-solo to install PostgreSQL, Python, and a web application inside of the guest.

You will probably notice that the configuration sections in the `Vagrantfile` look sort of like resources in Chef—this is because they both leverage Ruby blocks to configure their resources. So with Vagrant, in order to specify the provisioning mechanism being used, the `config.vm.provision` option is set to the desired tool. Here, we will use Chef-solo, which is named `"chef_solo"`; so, we will extend our `Vagrantfile` to indicate this:

```
Vagrant.configure("2") do |config|
  config.vm.box = "ubuntu/trusty64"
  config.vm.provision "chef_solo" do |chef|
    # ... Chef specific settings block
  end
end
```

Understanding the limitations of Chef-solo

For the most part, Chef-solo operates a lot like the traditional client-server mode of chef-client. The primary differences result from the fact that Chef-solo does not interact with a central Chef server and therefore lacks support for the following:

- Node data storage
- Search indexes
- Centralized distribution of cookbooks
- A centralized API that interacts with and integrates infrastructure components
- Authentication or authorization
- Persistent attributes

As a result, if you are writing recipes to be used with Chef-solo, you will be unable to rely on search for nodes, roles, or other data and may need to modify the way you find data for your recipes. You can still load data from data bags for complex data, but they will not be centrally located; rather, they will be located in a number of JSON files that contain the required data.

Configuring Chef-solo

There are a number of options available for the Chef-solo provisioner in Vagrant. For the most up-to-date documentation of Vagrant, be sure to visit the official Vagrant documentation site at `http://docs.vagrantup.com/v2/`.

Most of the configuration options are ways to provide paths to various Chef resources such as cookbooks, data bags, environments, recipes, and roles. Any paths specified are relative to the Vagrant workspace root (where the `Vagrantfile` is located); this is because these are mounted in the guest under `/vagrant` and are the only way to get data into the host during the bootstrap phase. The ones we will be using are:

- `cookbooks_path`: This consists of a single string or an array of paths to the location where cookbooks are stored. The default location is `cookbooks`.
- `data_bags_path`: This consists of a path to data bags' JSON files. The default path is `empty`.
- `roles_path`: This consists of an array or a single string of paths where roles are defined in JSON. The default value is `empty`.

In our case, we will be reusing our example cookbooks from the earlier chapter. You can fetch them from GitHub at `http://github.com/johnewart/chef_cookbook_files`; either download the ZIP file or clone them using Git locally. Once you have done that, copy `cookbooks`, `roles`, and `data_bags` from the archive to your Vagrant workspace. These will be the resources that you will use for your Vagrant image as well. In order to tell Vagrant's Chef-solo provider how to find these, we will update our `Vagrantfile` again to include the following configuration:

```
Vagrant.configure("2") do |config|
  config.vm.box = "ubuntu/trusty64"
  config.vm.provision "chef_solo" do |chef|
    chef.cookbooks_path = "cookbooks"
    chef.roles_path = "roles"
    chef.data_bags_path = "data_bags"
  end
end
```

Telling Chef-solo what to run

Inside of the `provision` block, we have a Chef object that effectively represents a Chef client run. This object has a number of methods (such as the path settings we already saw), one of which is the `add_recipe` method. This allows us to manually build our run list without requiring roles or data bags and can be used, as shown in the following example, to install the PostgreSQL server with no special configuration:

```
Vagrant.configure("2") do |config|
  config.vm.box = "ubuntu/trusty64"
  config.vm.provision "chef_solo" do |chef|
    chef.cookbooks_path = "cookbooks"
    chef.roles_path = "roles"
    chef.data_bags_path = "data_bags"
    # Build run list
    chef.add_recipe "postgresql::server"
  end
end
```

This will tell Vagrant that we want to use our defined directories to load our resources, and we want to add the `postgresql::server` recipe to our run list. Because cookbooks are by default expected to be in `[vagrant root]/cookbooks`, we can shorten this example as shown in the following code, as we are not yet using roles or data bags:

```
Vagrant.configure("2") do |config|
  config.vm.box = "ubuntu/trusty64"
  config.vm.provision "chef_solo" do |chef|
    chef.add_recipe "postgresql::server"
  end
end
```

Using roles and data bags with Chef-solo

As you are already aware by now, we may want to perform more complex configuration of our hosts. Let's take a look at how to use both roles and data bags as well as our cookbooks to deploy our Python web application into our Vagrant guest similar to how we deployed it to EC2:

```
Vagrant.configure("2") do |config|
  config.vm.box = "ubuntu/trusty64"
  config.vm.provision "chef_solo" do |chef|
    chef.cookbooks_path = "cookbooks"
    chef.roles_path = "roles"
    chef.data_bags_path = "data_bags"
    # Build run list
```

```
      chef.add_role("base_server")
      chef.add_role("postgresql_server")
      chef.add_role("web_server")
   end
end
```

Just like the `cookbooks` path, the roles path is relative to the project root if a relative path is given.

Injecting custom JSON data

Additional configuration data for Chef attributes can be passed into Chef-solo. This is done by setting the `json` property with a Ruby hash (dictionary-like object), which is converted to JSON and passed into Chef:

```
Vagrant.configure("2") do |config|
   config.vm.provision "chef_solo" do |chef|
     #  ...
     chef.json = {
        "apache" => {
           "listen_address" => "0.0.0.0"
        }
     }
   end
end
```

Hashes, arrays, and so on can be used with the JSON configuration object. Basically, anything that can be turned cleanly into JSON works.

Providing a custom node name

You can specify a custom node name by setting the `node_name` property. This is useful for cookbooks that may depend on this being set to some sort of value. For example:

```
Vagrant.configure("2") do |config|
   config.vm.provision "chef_solo" do |chef|
     chef.node_name = "db00"
   end
end
```

Getting to know the Chef shell

The Chef shell, previously called `shef`, provides an interactive tool or **read-eval-print-loop (REPL)** to work with Chef resources. Much in the same way IRB or any other language's REPL shell works, `chef-shell` is a way to interact with `knife`. This is handy for experimenting with resources while writing recipes so that you can see what happens interactively rather than having to upload your cookbook to a server and then executing the chef-client on a target node. Additionally, the Chef shell provides a resource to add breakpoints to recipe execution so that it can be used to debug recipe execution, which is a very handy feature.

Using the Chef shell

As of 11.x, `shef` has been replaced with `chef-shell` and can be used in three different modes: standalone, solo, and client mode. Each of these has a slightly different set of functionalities and expected use cases.

The standalone mode

The standalone mode is used to run Chef in an interactive mode with nothing loaded; this is almost like running an REPL such as `irb` or `python` on the command line. This is also the default behavior of `chef-shell` if nothing is specified.

The solo mode

The solo mode is invoked using the `-s` or `--solo` command-line flag and is a way to use chef-shell as a chef-solo client. It will load any cookbooks using the same mechanism that chef-solo users would, and it will use any chef-solo JSON file provided to it using the `-j` command-line option.

The following are examples of using the solo mode:

```
chef-shell -s
chef-shell -s -j /home/myuser/chef/chef-solo.json
```

The client mode

The client mode is enabled with the `-z` or `--client` command-line flag; this mode causes `chef-shell` to act as though you invoked chef-client on the host. The shell will read the local client configuration and perform the normal duties of chef-client: connecting to your Chef server and downloading any required run lists, attributes, and cookbooks. However, it will allow for interactive execution so that it is possible to debug or diagnose issues with recipes on the endhost. When using the client mode, you can use an alternate configuration file with the `-c` command-line option, or specify a different Chef server URL via the `-s` command-line option.

The example uses the following:

```
chef-shell --client -c /etc/chef/alternate.conf
chef-shell --client -s http://test.server.url:8080/
```

Interacting with the Chef server using the shell

The Chef shell provides you with the ability to interact with the server quickly in the same way you would use `knife`, but without the overhead of typing **knife search node...** or **knife node list**, and so on. It is a very convenient way to query the data stored in the Chef server interactively. In order to interact with the server from your workstation, you need to make sure that your shell's configuration file, located in `~/.chef/chef_shell.rb`, is configured properly. If you are connecting with `chef-shell` from a node, then the configuration in `/etc/chef/client.rb` (or similar on Windows) will be used instead.

This file, similar to the `knife.rb` or `client.rb` file, contains the required certificate data and configuration data to connect to the Chef server. An example configuration file will resemble the following, with paths, organization, and client names updated accordingly:

```
node_name              'myorg'
client_key             File.expand_path('~/.chef/client.pem')
validation_key         File.expand_path('~/.chef/validator.pem')
validation_client_name "myorg-validator"
chef_server_url    'https://api.opscode.com/organizations/myorg'
```

All of these files are present if your knife installation is operational, and the configuration file closely resembles that of knife.rb—if you need values for these on your workstation, take a look at the ~/.chef/knife.rb file. Once you have configured your shell, you can pass the -z command-line flag to connect as the chef-client would:

```
[jewart]% chef-shell -z
loading configuration: /Users/jewart/.chef/chef_shell.rb
Session type: client
Loading......resolving cookbooks for run list: []
Synchronizing Cookbooks:
done.


This is the chef-shell.
 Chef Version: 11.12.8
 http://www.opscode.com/chef
 http://docs.opscode.com/


run 'help' for help, 'exit' or ^D to quit.


Ohai2u jewart@!
chef >
```

Interacting with data

From here, you can interact with the Chef server in a variety of ways, including searching, modifying, and displaying any data elements (roles, nodes, data bags, environments, cookbooks, and clients), performing a client run (including stepping through it, one step at a time), assuming the identity of another node, and printing the attributes of the local node. For example, listing the roles on the Chef server can be performed with the roles.all method, shown as follows:

```
chef > roles.all
 => [role[umbraco_cms], role[umbraco], role[base_server], role[web_
server], role[postgresql_server]]
```

Searching your data

Searching the data elements is also supported, as each data type has a find method attached to it. The find method takes a map of the attribute and pattern to look for and returns the results. For example, you can find all roles on the Chef server that begin with "um" with the following command:

```
chef > umbraco_roles = roles.find(:name => "um*")
 => [role[umbraco_cms], role[umbraco]]
```

Editing your data

Any object in your Chef server can be edited directly from the Chef shell using the edit command from inside the shell. This will invoke your favorite editor to edit the raw JSON of the object in question, which provides a more direct mechanism over using knife (node|role|data bag) edit on the command line, as you can quickly manipulate a number of records a lot more easily. For example, to edit all of the roles that contain the name "apache" and save the results, you can use the following Ruby code:

```
chef > apache_roles = roles.find(:name => "*apache*")
> [... some list... ]
chef> apache_roles.each do |r|
chef>    updated = edit r
chef>    updated.save
chef> end
```

This will find all roles whose name contains "apache". Then for each record, edit the JSON, storing the results in variable named updated, and then save that record back to the Chef server.

Transforming data

In this way, you can interact with any of the resources that are available to you, allowing you to quickly find and manipulate any data stored in Chef directly using the Ruby code. For example, to find all clients with a given string in their name and disable their administrative access, you can use the following code:

```
clients.transform("*:*") do |client|
  if client.name =~ /bad_user/i
    client.admin(false)
    true
```

```
    else
       nil
    end
end
```

 Use `caution` when transforming your data from the Chef shell; it is an incredibly powerful tool, but its effects are destructive. These changes are not reversible (at least not without forethought or backups) and could damage your data if you are not careful. For example, if the previous code was transcribed incorrectly, it could potentially render all users unable to administer the system.

Executing recipes with Chef shell

Two great features of `chef-shell` are the ability to rewind a run (to step backwards) and to be able to step forward in the run one resource at a time. As an example, let's look at how to define a simple recipe in `chef-shell` interactively and then run it, start it over, and step through it.

First, let's fire up `chef-shell` with the following command:

```
[jewart]% chef-shell
loading configuration: none (standalone session)
Session type: standalone
Loading......done.

This is the chef-shell.
 Chef Version: 11.12.8
 http://www.opscode.com/chef
 http://docs.opscode.com/

run 'help' for help, 'exit' or ^D to quit.

Ohai2u jewart@!
chef >
```

The `chef-shell` prompt will change based on the state you are in. If you are working with a recipe, the prompt will change to be `chef:recipe >`.

Creating a recipe in the shell

The Chef shell has a number of modes—recipe mode and attribute mode. Recipe mode is activated when working with recipes and will be what we use here. In order to activate it, type `recipe_mode` at the prompt:

```
chef > recipe_mode

chef:recipe >
```

Here, we will create resources to create a file in the current directory interactively using a `file` resource with no associated configuration block, only the name:

```
chef:recipe > file "foo.txt"
 => <file[foo.txt] @name: "foo.txt" @noop: nil @before: nil @params: {}
@provider: Chef::Provider::File @allowed_actions: [:nothing, :create,
:delete, :touch, :create_if_missing] @action: "create" @updated: false
@updated_by_last_action: false @supports: {} @ignore_failure: false @
retries: 0 @retry_delay: 2 @source_line: "(irb#1):1:in 'irb_binding'" @
guard_interpreter: :default @elapsed_time: 0 @resource_name: :file @path:
"foo.txt" @backup: 5 @atomic_update: true @force_unlink: false @manage_
symlink_source: nil @diff: nil @sensitive: false @cookbook_name: nil @
recipe_name: nil>
```

One thing to note here is that the shell will print out the results of the last operation executed in the shell. This is part of an REPL shell's implicit behavior; it is the print part of REPL: input is read and evaluated, then the results are printed out, and the shell loops to wait for more input from the user. This can be controlled by enabling or disabling the echo state; `echo off` will prevent the printed output and `echo on` will turn it back on.

It is critical to note that, at this point, nothing has been executed; we have only described a `file` resource that will be acted upon if the recipe is run. You can verify this by making sure that there is no file named `foo.txt` in the directory you executed `chef-shell` from. The recipe can be run by issuing the `run_chef` command, which will execute all of the steps in the recipe from start to finish. Here is an example of this:

```
chef:recipe > run_chef

INFO: Processing file[foo.txt] action create ((irb#1) line 1)

DEBUG: touching foo.txt to create it

INFO: file[foo.txt] created file foo.txt

DEBUG: found current_mode == nil, so we are creating a new file, updating
mode
```

```
DEBUG: found current_mode == nil, so we are creating a new file, updating
mode
DEBUG: found current_uid == nil, so we are creating a new file, updating
owner
DEBUG: found current_gid == nil, so we are creating a new file, updating
group
DEBUG: found current_uid == nil, so we are creating a new file, updating
owner
INFO: file[foo.txt] owner changed to 501
DEBUG: found current_gid == nil, so we are creating a new file, updating
group
INFO: file[foo.txt] group changed to 20
DEBUG: found current_mode == nil, so we are creating a new file, updating
mode
INFO: file[foo.txt] mode changed to 644
DEBUG: selinux utilities can not be found. Skipping selinux permission
fixup.
```

Defining node attributes

Just as in any recipe, attributes can be used in the recipes defined in the shell. However, in the standalone mode, there will be no attributes defined initially; solo and client modes will likely have attributes defined by their JSON file or the Chef server, respectively. In order to interact with the currently defined attributes, we must switch between the recipe mode and attribute mode. This is achieved using the attributes_mode command as shown in the following code:

```
chef:recipe > attributes_mode
chef:attributes >
```

Here we can perform two primary operations: getting and setting node attributes. These are ways of modifying the values that are accessed from inside the node Mash in a recipe.

> Remember that the node's attributes are accessed as a Mash, a key-insensitive hash that allows you to interchange string keys with symbol keys. The Mash class is not a built-in structure in Ruby—it is provided by Chef for convenience so that hash keys can be either symbols or strings and have the same effect.

Setting attributes

Setting attributes is achieved using the `set` command, which has the following form:

```
set[:key] = value
```

Here, `:key` can be a single-level key or a multilevel key similar to any entry in the `attributes/default.rb` file. As an example, we can construct an application configuration using the following:

```
set[:webapp][:path] = "/opt/webapp"
set[:webapp][:db][:username] = "dbuser"
set[:webapp][:db][:password] = "topsecret"
set[:webapp][:user] = "webuser"
set[:postgresql][:config][:listen] = "0.0.0.0"
```

Any parent keys that are non-existent are implicitly created on the fly, so you do not need to do something like the following:

```
set[:webapp] = {}
set[:webapp][:path] = "/opt/webapp"
```

Accessing attributes

In order to display an attribute when in the attributes mode, simply type in the name of the key you are interested in. For example, if you had executed the set commands listed previously, then asking for the `webapp` hash is as simple as typing `webapp`, as follows:

```
chef:attributes > webapp
 => {"path"=>"/opt/webapp", "db"=>{"username"=>"dbuser",
"password"=>"topsecret"}, "user"=>"webuser"}
```

However, if you wish to access these when in the recipe mode, they are accessed through the `node` hash, as shown here:

```
chef:attributes > recipe_mode
 => :attributes
chef:recipe > node[:webapp]
 => {"path"=>"/opt/webapp", "db"=>{"username"=>"dbuser",
"password"=>"topsecret"}, "user"=>"webuser"}
```

They can be used via the `node` hash in just the same way you would use them in a recipe. If you want to construct a file block that created a `foo.txt` file located in the install path of our `webapp` hash, you can easily use the following example inside your shell:

```
file "#{node[:webapp][:path]}/foo.txt"
```

This makes writing recipes using the interactive shell feel exactly the same as writing recipe files.

Using configuration blocks

A resource in a recipe file can have a Ruby block with attributes, and you can do this in `chef-shell` in exactly the same fashion. Simply insert `do` after the resource name and the shell will behave as a multiline editor, allowing you to complete the block. The following example demonstrates providing a content attribute to a `file` resource in this manner:

```
chef:recipe > file "not_empty.txt" do
chef:recipe > content "Not empty!"
chef:recipe ?> end
 => <file[not_empty.txt] @name: "not_empty.txt" @noop: nil @before: nil @
params: {} @provider: Chef::Provider::File @allowed_actions: [:nothing,
:create, :delete, :touch, :create_if_missing] @action: "create" @updated:
false @updated_by_last_action: false @supports: {} @ignore_failure: false
@retries: 0 @retry_delay: 2 @source_line: "(irb#1):2:in 'irb_binding'" @
guard_interpreter: :default @elapsed_time: 0 @resource_name: :file @path:
"not_empty.txt" @backup: 5 @atomic_update: true @force_unlink: false @
manage_symlink_source: nil @diff: nil @sensitive: false @cookbook_name:
nil @recipe_name: nil @content: "Not empty!">
```

Note that when the shell printed out the previous `file` resource, `@content` was not present. Here, everything but the name remains the same, and there is an additional property inside the object, `@content`, as specified in our attributes block.

Interactively executing recipes

Running a recipe step by step is a good way of slowing down the execution of a recipe so that the state of the system can be inspected before proceeding with the next resource. This can be incredibly useful both for debugging (as will be discussed later) and for developing and exploring resources. It gives you a chance to see what has happened and what side effects your recipe has as the recipe is executed. To achieve this, the Chef shell allows you to *rewind* your recipe to the start and run from the beginning, execute your recipe one *step* at a time, and *resume* execution from the current point to the end.

Restarting our Chef shell, let's take a look at how we can use this:

```
recipe_mode
echo off
file "foo.txt"
file "foo.txt" do
  action :delete
end
file "foo.txt" do
  content "Foo content"
end
```

Here our recipe is quite simple—create an empty file, `foo.txt`, remove it, and then recreate it with "Foo content". If we execute our recipe using `run_chef`, the shell will perform all the operations in one pass without stopping and will not allow us to check whether the delete action occurred. Instead, we can run our recipe and then rewind and use the `chef_run.step` method to interactively walk through our recipe:

```
chef:recipe > run_chef
... execution output ...
chef:recipe > echo on
 => true
chef:recipe > chef_run.rewind
 => 0
chef:recipe > chef_run.step
INFO: Processing file[foo.txt] action create ((irb#1) line 3)
 => 1
chef:recipe > chef_run.step
INFO: Processing file[foo.txt] action delete ((irb#1) line 4)
INFO: file[foo.txt] backed up to /var/chef/backup/foo.txt.chef-
20140615175124.279917
file[foo.txt] deleted file at foo.txt
 => 2
chef:recipe > chef_run.step
INFO: Processing file[foo.txt] action create ((irb#1) line 7)
INFO: file[foo.txt] created file foo.txt
INFO: file[foo.txt] updated file contents foo.txt
```

```
INFO: file[foo.txt] owner changed to 501
INFO: file[foo.txt] group changed to 20
INFO: file[foo.txt] mode changed to 644
 => 3
```

As you can see, here we were able to rewind our recipe back to the first instruction (position 0, as the result of `chef_run.rewind` indicates), and then walk through each resource step by step using `chef_run.step` and see what happened. During this run, you can easily open a terminal after you rewind the recipe, delete the `foo.txt` file from the previous run, and check that initially there is no `foo.txt` file, then step through the next command in the recipe, validate that there is an empty `foo.txt` file, and so on. This is a very good way to learn how resources work and to see what they do without having to formalize your recipe in a cookbook, provision and bootstrap a host, and so on.

Debugging with the Chef shell

Debugging is achieved in two different ways using `chef-shell`: stepping interactively through a recipe or using a special breakpoint resource that is only used by `chef-shell`. Running recipes interactively step by step is good to build recipes locally; experiment with resources to determine the effect of certain attributes, actions and notifications; or to inspect the state of the system after each resource has been acted upon. The breakpoints allow you to inject very specific stopping points into the client run so that the world can be inspected before continuing. Typically, once a breakpoint is encountered, you will want to step through the execution of your script (at least for a while) so that these are not mutually exclusive techniques.

Using the breakpoint resource

The breakpoint resource is structured just like any other Chef resource. The resource's name attribute is the location where you want to insert the breakpoint, and it has only one action, `:break`, which signals `chef-shell` to interrupt execution of the current recipe and provide an interactive shell. Any breakpoint resources in recipes are ignored by the chef-client. That way, if they are forgotten about and left in a recipe, they will not cause havoc in production. That being said, they should only be used when actively debugging an issue and removed before releasing your recipes into your production environment.

The name attribute has the following structure:

```
when resource resource_name
```

Here, when has the value of "before" or "after", to indicate whether the breakpoint should stop before or after execution, respectively and resource is the type of resource that when combined with resource_name is the unique identifier that will trigger the breakpoint. For example:

```
before file '/tmp/foo.txt'
```

This would cause the shell to interrupt execution of the recipes immediately before any file resource that was manipulating /tmp/foo.txt. Another example, where we want to stop execution after installing the git package, would look like the following:

```
after package 'git'
```

Using this, we will tell chef-shell that execution was to be paused once the git package was modified. Let's look at how we can form a simple recipe complete with breakpoint resources that would use these examples:

```
breakpoint "before file '/tmp/foo.txt'" do
  action :break
end

breakpoint "after package 'git'" do
  action :break
end

file '/tmp/foo.txt' do
  action :create
end

package 'git' do
  action :remove
end
```

For those who have used gdb or any other debugger, this will be easy to understand; if you have not used an interactive debugger, then try a few of the interactive examples, and you will get the hang of it in no time at all.

Chef shell provides a comprehensive way to interact with your recipes. Now that you see how to test out and debug your work, let's take a look at how we can go one step further in our testing to perform full end-to-end integration testing of our infrastructure.

Integration testing

With integration testing, your tests move into testing beyond your code. With ChefSpec, we looked at how to verify that a recipe was executing statements as expected. However, unit testing has its limits; integration testing completes the picture by testing cookbooks in conjunction with real hosts that run the desired operating system(s):

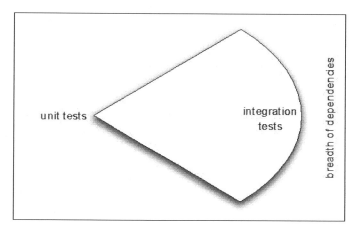

This means testing cookbooks from the outside rather than from the inside, where a unit test provides very narrow testing of code inside of cookbooks, integration tests perform deployment of your cookbooks in a test-specific environment and then execute probes to validate that the system is in the desired state. One of the most popular tools for this is **Test Kitchen**, which we will take a brief tour of.

Using Test Kitchen

Test Kitchen is an open source tool that helps to automate integration testing of Chef cookbooks. Where a ChefSpec test would validate that a `file` resource was called during an execution, a similarly tasked Test Kitchen test would spin up a new instance, execute your recipe(s), and then validate that the file was actually created on all platforms that you expect the recipe to work on. One of the great things about Test Kitchen is that it supports a number of different **driver** plugins to manage your target hosts, including Vagrant (the default), EC2, OpenStack, Docker, and Rackspace Cloud among others. This enables you to test your cookbooks not only on local virtual machines using Vagrant, but to verify that they work correctly on a cloud service as well. The ability to perform integration tests on different types of hosts brings your tests that much closer to matching a production environment, thereby increasing your confidence in the changes you are making.

Installing Test Kitchen

Currently, Test Kitchen is distributed as a Ruby gem, so installation is quite straightforward:

```
gem install test-kitchen
```

By installing this gem, you are also installing a command-line tool, `kitchen`, which is used to interact with Test Kitchen. Similar to Vagrant, Bundler, and other tools, Test Kitchen uses a configuration file to store information about what to test, where to test it (on what virtual machines), and how to test it.

Testing with Test Kitchen

As mentioned before, Test Kitchen focuses on integration testing of your Chef components. This means that it needs to be able to execute your recipes on a host (or a set of hosts) and then invoke a set of tests to validate that the expected behavior occurred on the endhost(s). Test Kitchen is responsible for the following:

- Provisioning a clean host for testing
- Installing Chef onto the new host
- Executing our recipes on the host
- Validating the behavior of the recipes on the host

So, let's get started with some actual testing!

Building a simple cookbook

In order to demonstrate how to use Test Kitchen, we will need to write a cookbook that we can run on our test hosts and write tests to validate the behavior. In order to focus on how to use Test Kitchen, we will take a look at a very simple cookbook that just creates a file on the host filesystem so that it is guaranteed that it will work on both Ubuntu and CentOS platforms.

First, create a place to do your work:

```
mkdir -p testfile-cookbook/recipes
```

Then, add a very simple `metadata.rb` in your `testfile-cookbook` directory with the following contents inside:

```
name "testfile"
version "1.0"
```

Once that is complete, add a default recipe, `recipes/default.rb`, with the sample recipe code as follows:

```
file "/tmp/myfile.txt" do
  content "My awesome file!"
end
```

Now that we have a complete (albeit simple) cookbook, let's take a look at how to test it using Test Kitchen.

Preparing your cookbook for the kitchen

In order to start using Test Kitchen, you will need to prepare your test environment. Test Kitchen relies on a configuration file, `.kitchen.yml`, to tell it what to do. You can generate it by hand, or you could use the `init` command as part of the `kitchen` tool:

kitchen init

This will do a few things for you: first, it will create a `.kitchen.yml` file with some sane defaults in the current directory. Then, it will create a `test/integration/default` directory for your integration tests, and then it will install the Vagrant driver for Test Kitchen so that it can interact with Vagrant virtual machines (if it has not already been installed).

If you look at the `.kitchen.yml` file, you will see that the initial file contains the following YAML code:

```
---
driver:
  name: vagrant

provisioner:
  name: chef_solo

platforms:
  - name: ubuntu-12.04
  - name: centos-6.4

suites:
  - name: default
    run_list:
      - recipe[testfile::default]
    attributes:
```

This configuration file instructs Test Kitchen to use Vagrant to manage the target instances and to use Chef-solo for provisioning, and it should execute the default suite of tests on both Ubuntu 12.04 and CentOS 6.4. Of course, you can always modify or extend this list if you have other systems that you want to run tests on, but this is a reasonable default list for now.

Notice that we don't have any attributes specified as our default recipe and it does not use attributes. If you need to provide attributes to test recipes, this would be the place to do it, which is laid out as a dictionary in YAML. Each test suite has its own run list and defined attributes that allow you to check the behavior of a variety of configuration data and recipe combinations.

Testing your new cookbook

Testing a cookbook with Test Kitchen is outlined in the following three steps:

1. Provisioning a host if needed.
2. Converging the host so that it is up to date.
3. Executing tests.

Let's take a look at how we will perform these with our simple cookbook to check that it works properly.

Provisioning the instance

Before you can test, you will need to prepare the instances for testing—this is done using the `kitchen create <instance name>` command. Only you don't know what instance to bring up just yet. To get the list of instances that can be run, we will use the `list` subcommand:

```
[jewart]$ kitchen list
Instance              Driver    Provisioner   Last Action
default-ubuntu-1204   Vagrant   ChefSolo      <Not Created>
default-centos-64     Vagrant   ChefSolo      <Not Created>
```

You will see that this list is generated by a combination of the platforms and the suites listed in the `.kitchen.yml` file. If you were to define a new suite, named `server`, then your list would include two additional instances, `server-ubuntu-1204` and `server-centos-64`.

Once you have seen this list, you can create an Ubuntu 12.04 instance with the following command:

```
kitchen create default-ubuntu-1204
```

This will use Vagrant and VirtualBox to provision a new headless Ubuntu 12.04 host and boot it up for you to start testing with. If you don't already have an Ubuntu 12.04 Vagrant image downloaded, then it will be downloaded for you automatically (this is a large image so it may take a while to complete this operation, depending on your connection speed, if you are following along).

This will look familiar to those that used Vagrant at the beginning of the chapter:

```
[jewart]% kitchen create default-ubuntu-1204
-----> Starting Kitchen (v1.2.1)
-----> Creating <default-ubuntu-1204>...


 Provisioning happens...


       Finished creating <default-ubuntu-1204> (4m2.59s).
-----> Kitchen is finished. (4m2.83s)
```

However, this only builds the virtual machine for our tests; it does not run our recipes or our tests in the newly constructed host. Before we move on to writing a test, let's take a look at how to run our recipe inside our instance.

Converging the newly created instance

The next step is to execute our run list ("converge" in Chef parlance) on the new instance. This is done with Test Kitchen's `converge` command and can be used for all or one specific instance. In order to converge our Ubuntu 12.04 instance, the following command is used:

```
kitchen converge default-ubuntu-1204
```

What this will do is transfer any required data files, install Chef as needed, and then execute the run list for the specified suite (`default` in this case) on the instance. Here is a sample run of `converge` (with some parts removed):

```
[jewart]% kitchen converge  default-ubuntu-1204
-----> Starting Kitchen (v1.2.1)
-----> Converging <default-ubuntu-1204>...
       Preparing files for transfer
       Preparing current project directory as a cookbook
       Removing non-cookbook files before transfer
```

```
-----> Installing Chef Omnibus (true)


Installation of Chef happens...


Compiling Cookbooks...
Converging 1 resources
Recipe: testfile::default
```

And then you will see the output of a normal Chef run after that—at this point, the run list is complete and the instance has been converged to the latest state. Now that it's been converged, we will continue to write a very simple test to verify that our recipe did the right thing.

Writing a simple test

Tests are stored in a directory whose structure is similar to other Chef components—the directory we created previously with kitchen init, tests/integration/ default, allows us to keep our integration tests separate from spec tests or other types of tests. The integration directory will contain one directory per suite so that test files are grouped together based on the particular component or aspect of your cookbook that is being tested. Additionally, depending on the type of the test framework being used, your tests will be contained in another child directory for the given suite. In this case, we will take a look at the **BASH Automated Testing System (BATS)**, so our test will be placed in the tests/integration/default/bats/file_ created.bats file and will look like the following code:

```
#!/usr/bin/env bats


@test "myfile.txt exists in /tmp" {
  [ -f "/tmp/myfile.txt" ]
}
```

This allows us to use the simple -f BASH test (which returns true if the specified value exists) to guarantee that the file was created on the instance.

Next, we can run this test with kitchen verify default-ubuntu-1204 and see that the BATS plugin was installed and that our test was executed and passed:

```
[jewart]% kitchen verify default-ubuntu-1204
-----> Starting Kitchen (v1.2.1)
-----> Setting up <default-ubuntu-1204>...
Fetching: thor-0.19.0.gem (100%)
Fetching: busser-0.6.2.gem (100%)
```

```
Successfully installed thor-0.19.0
Successfully installed busser-0.6.2
2 gems installed
-----> Setting up Busser
        Creating BUSSER_ROOT in /tmp/busser
        Creating busser binstub
        Plugin bats installed (version 0.2.0)
-----> Running postinstall for bats plugin
Installed Bats to /tmp/busser/vendor/bats/bin/bats
        Finished setting up <default-ubuntu-1204> (0m8.94s).
-----> Verifying <default-ubuntu-1204>...
        Suite path directory /tmp/busser/suites does not exist, skipping.
Uploading /tmp/busser/suites/bats/file_created.bats (mode=0644)
-----> Running bats test suite
 √ myfile.txt exists in /tmp


1 test, 0 failures
        Finished verifying <default-ubuntu-1204> (0m0.67s).
-----> Kitchen is finished. (0m9.86s)
```

To demonstrate what happens if the file does not exist, we can clone our test to create a second simple test that validates the existence of /tmp/myotherfile.txt, and run our verify command again without making a corresponding change to our recipe. The output from Test Kitchen will tell us that our test failed and why:

```
-----> Running bats test suite
 √ myfile.txt exists in /tmp
 ✗ myotherfile.txt exists in /tmp
    (in test file /tmp/busser/suites/bats/other_file.bats, line 4)


2 tests, 1 failure
Command [/tmp/busser/vendor/bats/bin/bats /tmp/busser/suites/bats] exit
code was 1
>>>>>> Verify failed on instance <default-ubuntu-1204>.
```

Combining all the steps

Fortunately, the fine folks that created Test Kitchen realized that it would be tedious to run all three steps every time you wanted to run some tests. As a result, there is the `kitchen test` command that will provision an instance, execute the run list, verify the results, and then tear down the instance with only one command. In this case, you can replace them with the following single command:

```
kitchen test default-ubuntu-1204
```

This covers the basics of testing your cookbooks with Test Kitchen. There are other things that can be done with Test Kitchen, including using other testing mechanisms, testing cookbook dependencies, validating whether services are running, fully automating Test Kitchen as part of your release process, and plenty more. For more information, visit the project at `http://kitchen.ci/`.

Extending Chef

Chef is developed in the open with flexibility and extensibility in mind. Most of the tools are architected to support loading custom plugins to support development of add-ons for new functionality. As you saw earlier, Knife's cloud service support is provided by plugins, one for each cloud service, including EC2, Azure, and Rackspace cloud. We will look at how that happens so that you can explore writing your own plugins for Knife, Ohai, and other Chef components should the need arise.

In addition to extending Chef's core components directly, it is possible to extend the functionality of your Chef ecosystem by building enhancements to existing tools that can leverage Chef's data APIs to provide data about your infrastructure.

Writing an Ohai plugin

Ohai (a play on the phrase oh, hi!) is a tool that is used to detect attributes on a node, and provide these attributes to the chef-client at the start of every `chef-client` run. Without Ohai, the `chef-client` will not function, and therefore, it must be present on a node in order for Chef to work. The data that is collected is authoritative—it has the highest level of precedence when computing attribute data for client runs on a node.

The types of attributes that Ohai might be used for include:

- Platform details
- Network usage
- Memory usage
- Processor usage

- Kernel data
- Host names
- Information about the network topology
- Cloud-specific information

Ohai implements an extensible architecture through plugins that allows end users to write custom extensions to report information that is collected about a node. For example, there are plugins for EC2 cloud hosts that use EC2-specific mechanisms to determine information about the host, including its internal IP address and other bits of information.

This is incredibly useful for integrating Chef with an existing infrastructure, as you can automatically probe for local configuration data and generate attributes from that data. Once this data is stored in Chef, it can be used in search queries, recipes, and everywhere else that you could otherwise use node attributes.

Every Ohai plugin follows a pattern: it registers itself as providing a certain class of attribute data and contains a combination of general purpose and data collection methods to gather information about the local state of the system and report it back to the Chef server. Ohai already has built-in collectors for a number of platforms, including Linux, Windows, and BSD.

A sample Ohai plugin would look like the following:

```
Ohai.plugin(:Region) do
  provides "region"

  def init
    region Mash.new
  end

  collect_data(:default) do
    # Runs on all hosts whose platform is not specifically handled
    init
    region[:name] = "unknown"
  end

  collect_data(:linux, :freebsd) do
    # Run only on Linux and FreeBSD hosts
    init
    region[:name] = discover_region_unix
  end

  collect_data(:windows) do
```

```
    # Run on Windows hosts
    init
    region[:public_ip] = discover_region_windows
  end

  end
```

Here we register our plugin as providing a `region` data, there is an `init` method that creates a Mash for our `region` data, and a few data collection callbacks. Each data collection callback is registered as a block that is called for the specified platform(s). In our case, there are three callbacks registered, one for Windows systems, one for Linux and FreeBSD systems, and then a fallback that will be called for any platform not explicitly handled.

A note about writing Ohai plugins

The way we declare the `region` Mash in our `init` method is a little bit different than normal variable assignment in Ruby. In our plugin, we define the plugin's `region` property with the following code:

```
region Mash.new
```

On the surface, this might look like someone forgot an equals sign, as in the following Ruby code:

```
region = Mash.new
```

However, if there were an equals sign, the plugin would not work as intended. In this case, there is no equals sign missing and the code is correct. This is because Ohai's `Plugin` class leverages a special Ruby mechanism for intercepting calls to nonexistent methods and dynamically handling them. This mechanism is recognizable by the presence of a special method named `method_missing` in the code. In this case, the `method_missing` handler will call a special Ohai plugin method, `get_attribute`, if no arguments are passed, or it will call the `set_attribute` method if arguments are passed.

To demonstrate why this is used, if you wanted to have the same effect without the `method_missing` mechanism, then the plugin's `init` method could be written as:

```
def init
  set_attribute "region", Mash.new
end
```

Were you to do this, then our subsequent collect data methods would need to be rewritten as well. Here is an example of what they might look like:

```
collect_data(:platform) do
  init
  region = get_attribute "region"
  region[:name] = get_data_mechanism
  set_attribute "region", region
end
```

You can see that the `method_missing` mechanism makes writing plugins more natural, though it takes a little bit of extra work to understand how to write them at first.

Chef with Capistrano

One example of extending Chef through external tools is the `capistrano-chef` gem that extends the popular deployment tool, Capistrano. Written in Ruby, Capistrano was designed to deploy applications and perform light systems administration. If you have existing applications that are being deployed using Capistrano, this is an example of how to leverage your configuration data stored in Chef to make integration as seamless as possible.

If you have an existing application that uses Capistrano, you will have a `deploy.rb` file that defines the various application roles. Each tool has an array of IP addresses to hosts that provide that role and might look something like this:

```
role :web, '10.0.0.2', '10.0.0.3'
role :db, '10.0.0.2', :primary => true
```

By using `capistrano-chef`, you can do this:

```
require 'capistrano/chef'
chef_role :web,'roles:web'
chef_role :db, 'roles:database_master',
              :primary   => true,
              :attribute => :private_ip,
              :limit     => 1
```

Notice that here we have used a simple search query to determine the hosts that should be included in each Capistrano role. In this case, the `:web` role has been replaced with a Chef search query for all nodes that have the `web` Chef role associated with them. This allows you to model your data in Chef, but still use Capistrano to deploy your application stack, increasing the ease of integration.

This works because all of Chef's data is available via an HTTP API making integration as simple as making HTTP calls and parsing some JSON results (which, compared to some other integration mechanisms, is incredibly easy).

Automation and integration

One of the best parts about Chef is that your infrastructure and software model is consistent with what is deployed. What this means for you is that when chef-client runs on an endhost, that host's state is updated to match your modeled environment. For example, consider a scenario where you have 10 EC2 database hosts, and all of them have a special role, `database_server`, applied to them. This role's attributes indicate that PostgreSQL 9.1 is to be installed and its data should be stored in `/opt/postgresql/data`. By executing `chef-client` on all ten nodes, they will have PostgreSQL 9.1 installed and storing data in `/opt/postgresql/data`. Now consider that all of our nodes need to have a new EBS storage device attached to each of them, and PostgreSQL needs to be pointed to our new EBS device. Updating our model to include a recipe that mounts the EBS device gracefully shuts down PostgreSQL, moves the database data, reconfigures PostgreSQL, and starts it up again. We can automate and roll out this configuration to our fleet of ten database hosts. You can easily imagine ten hosts growing to hundreds or even thousands. This is what the power of automation is all about.

Automated updates and deployments

If you have confidence in your model and your cookbooks, then you can take this automation one step further. By automating the execution of `chef-client` on a periodic schedule, you can fully automate updates without needing to SSH into the hosts to run `chef-client`. However, this level of automation requires a high level of confidence in the correctness of your cookbooks. Achieving this requires continuous and in-depth testing of not only the code in the cookbooks developed but also of the dependencies that are needed to make your cookbooks work. To that end, comprehensive integration tests can help to build the confidence needed to move into a fully automated world.

Summary

By now you have been exposed to a lot of what Chef has to offer the DevOps community. You have seen what Chef does, how to install it, and how it works. Throughout this book, you have been introduced to some new ways of thinking about how to model infrastructure and use automated tools to manage it.

At this point, you hopefully understand how to model your infrastructure with Chef as well as install the various components related to Chef, ranging from the server to the client. From here, you can take what you've learned about the various components of Chef and use that information to build more advanced cookbooks to deploy your software and manage your infrastructure, ranging from cloud hosts to physical on-site hardware and even virtual machines using Vagrant. Once you have gotten things working, you can automate your configuration tools and ensure the reliability of your cookbooks through unit and integration tests as well.

Now, it is your turn to take this information and your new skills to automate your systems infrastructure in order to build exciting new things!

Index

default action 77
default behavior, resource
  overriding 77
definitions, cookbook support
    files 65, 85, 86
dependencies
  installing 119
  managing 120
  managing, in Chef 119
deployment keys, SSH keys
  adding 142, 143
deploy users 142
directories
  preparing 116, 117
domain-specific language (DSL) 65
driver plugins 181
dry-run mode 152

E

EC2 instances
  database host, configuring 127
  provisioning 126
echo off state 174
echo on state 174
encryption key
  storing, on nodes 156
environment
  about 29
  example 43
equal sign 81
ERB primer
  about 80
  Ruby code, executing 80
  URL 80

F

fetch_from_s3 method 152

G

gems
  managing, with Ruby Version
    Manager (RVM) 9
gemset 10

H

host
  provisioning, with Vagrant 162, 163

I

Image-O-Rama 35
image-processing role
  defining 32
image search role
  defining 32
infrastructure modeling
  about 29-31
  Chef, using 30
  environment 43, 44
  nodes, converging 42
  recipes, applying to role 37
  recipes, determining 35
  role 31
  role, implementing 34
  role, mapping to node 40-42
  service-oriented architecture,
    advantages 30
  service-oriented web application,
    services 30
  steps 29
installation, Chef server
  about 13
  components 14
  omnibus installer, obtaining 15
  on Red Hat Enterprise Linux 16
  on Ubuntu 15
  requisites 13
instance, Amazon EC2
  bootstrapping 54, 55
  provisioning 53, 54
  terminating 55, 56
instance, Rackspace Cloud
  provisioning 57-59
  terminating 59, 60
integration, Chef 192
integration testing
  about 181
  Test Kitchen, using 181

K

knife node list 170
knife plugin, Amazon EC2
  installing 52
knife-rackspace plugin 57
knife tool
  about 21, 51
  used, for searching data bags 157

L

load_current_resource method 153
local environment
  configuring 111

M

Mash, Chef 70
matching ChefSpec test
  creating 99
metadata 71, 72
mock methods 95
multiple attribute files
  about 68
  external attributes, loading 69
  multiple platforms, supporting 69
multiple machines
  managing, with search queries 159
mysql 114

N

node
  about 7, 27
  converging 42
  role, mapping to 40, 41
node attributes
  accessing 176, 177
  defining 175
  setting 176
node delete command 61
node hash 70

O

Ohai plugin
  attributes 188

writing 188-190
omnibus installation package, Chef 13
omnibus installer, Chef server
  obtaining 15
  outline 15
  steps 15
OpenSSH service role
  defining 33

P

PIP
  used, for writing definition 143-146
PostgreSQL service role
  defining 33
provider
  about 29, 65, 149
  implementing 150, 152
Python application
  modeling 111, 112
Python's requirements file
  using 120
Python virtual environment
  constructing 117, 118

R

Rackspace Cloud
  about 56, 57
  Chef node, removing 61
  instance, provisioning 57-59
  instance, terminating 59, 60
read-eval-print-loop (REPL) 169
recipe
  about 8, 28, 65, 74,
  applying, to role 37-39
  building 101
  cookbook, installing 36
  complicated recipe, actions 90-92
  creating, in Chef shell 174
  data bags, searching from 157
  determining 35
  developing 87, 88
  enhancing, with search method 136
  executing 88, 89
  failures 102, 103
  need for 35

Thank you for buying
Chef Essentials

About Packt Publishing

Packt, pronounced 'packed', published its first book "*Mastering phpMyAdmin for Effective MySQL Management*" in April 2004 and subsequently continued to specialize in publishing highly focused books on specific technologies and solutions.

Our books and publications share the experiences of your fellow IT professionals in adapting and customizing today's systems, applications, and frameworks. Our solution based books give you the knowledge and power to customize the software and technologies you're using to get the job done. Packt books are more specific and less general than the IT books you have seen in the past. Our unique business model allows us to bring you more focused information, giving you more of what you need to know, and less of what you don't.

Packt is a modern, yet unique publishing company, which focuses on producing quality, cutting-edge books for communities of developers, administrators, and newbies alike. For more information, please visit our website: www.packtpub.com.

About Packt Open Source

In 2010, Packt launched two new brands, Packt Open Source and Packt Enterprise, in order to continue its focus on specialization. This book is part of the Packt Open Source brand, home to books published on software built around Open Source licenses, and offering information to anybody from advanced developers to budding web designers. The Open Source brand also runs Packt's Open Source Royalty Scheme, by which Packt gives a royalty to each Open Source project about whose software a book is sold.

Writing for Packt

We welcome all inquiries from people who are interested in authoring. Book proposals should be sent to author@packtpub.com. If your book idea is still at an early stage and you would like to discuss it first before writing a formal book proposal, contact us; one of our commissioning editors will get in touch with you.

We're not just looking for published authors; if you have strong technical skills but no writing experience, our experienced editors can help you develop a writing career, or simply get some additional reward for your expertise.

Instant Chef Starter

ISBN: 978-1-78216-346-6   Paperback: 70 pages

A practical guide to getting started with Chef, an indispensable tool for provisioning and managing your system's infrastructure

1. Learn something new in an Instant!
   A short, fast, focused guide delivering immediate results.

2. Learn the core capabilities of Chef and how it integrates with your infrastructure.

3. Set up your own Chef server for managing your infrastructure.

4. Provision new servers with ease and develop your own recipes for use with Chef.

Configuration Management with Chef-Solo

ISBN: 978-1-78398-246-2   Paperback: 116 pages

A comprehensive guide to get you up and running with Chef-Solo

1. Explore various techniques that will help you save time in Infrastructure management.

2. Use the power of Chef-Solo to run your servers and configure and deploy applications in an automated manner.

3. This book will help you to understand the need for the configuration management tool and will provide you with a step-by-step guide to maintain your existing infrastructure.

Please check **www.PacktPub.com** for information on our titles

Managing Windows Servers with Chef

ISBN: 978-1-78398-242-4   Paperback: 110 pages

Harness the power of Chef to automate management of Windows-based systems using hands-on examples

1. Discover how Chef can be used to manage a heterogeneous network of Windows and Linux systems with ease.

2. Configure an entire .NET application stack, deploy it, and scale in the cloud.

3. Employ a step-by-step and practical approach to automate provisioning and configuration of Windows hosts with Chef.

Chef Infrastructure Automation Cookbook

ISBN: 978-1-84951-922-9   Paperback: 276 pages

Over 80 delicious recipes to automate your cloud and server infrastructure with Chef

1. Configure, deploy, and scale your applications.

2. Automate error prone and tedious manual tasks.

3. Manage your servers on-site or in the cloud.

4. Solve real world automation challenges with task-based recipes.

5. The book is filled with working code and easy-to-follow, step-by-step instructions.

Please check **www.PacktPub.com** for information on our titles